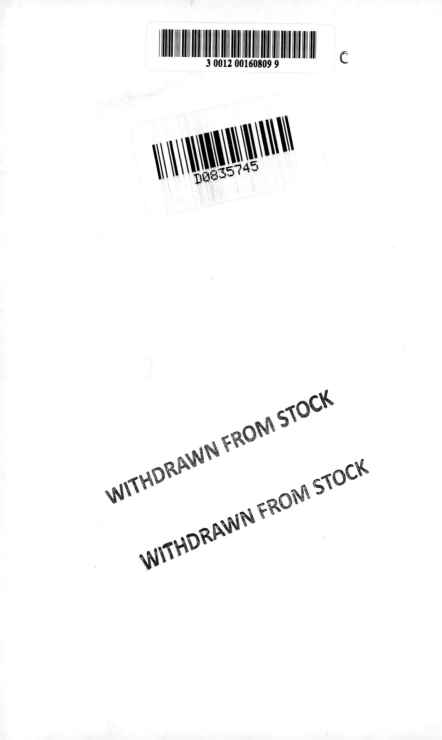

3 0012 00160809 9

C

D0835745

THE MAGNIFICENT SEVEN

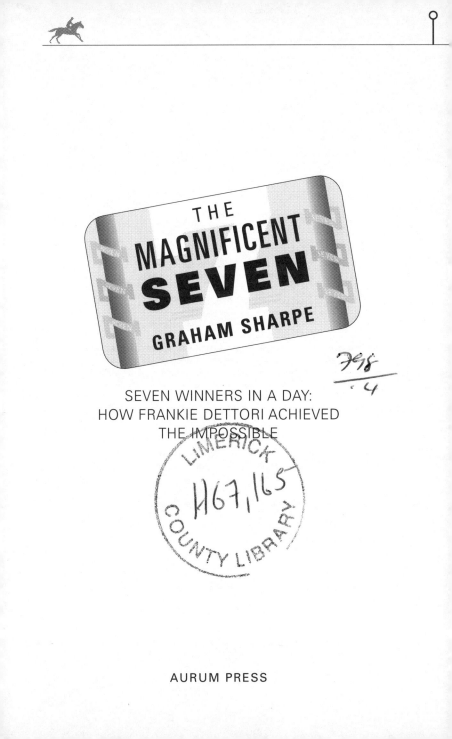

THE MAGNIFICENT SEVEN

GRAHAM SHARPE

SEVEN WINNERS IN A DAY:
HOW FRANKIE DETTORI ACHIEVED
THE IMPOSSIBLE

AURUM PRESS

First published in Great Britain
2001 by Aurum Press Ltd
25 Bedford Avenue, London WC1B 3AT

Design by Roger Hammond

A catalogue record for this book is available from the British Library.

ISBN 1 85410 800 X

1   3   5   7   9   10   8   6   4   2
2001   2003   2005   2004   2002

Typeset by M Rules
Printed in Great Britain by MPG Books Ltd, Bodmin

To my long suffering family –
Sheila, Steeven and Paul.

I couldn't have written this book without
your tolerance. Thanks and love.

CHAPTER ONE

'I COULD HAVE AN EACH-WAY CHANCE IN THE FIRST, AND I MAY WIN THE THIRD'

FRANKIE DETTORI

DEREK HEENEY ROSE EARLY on 28 September 1996. As a lad in Michael Stoute's famous Freemason Lodge stables in Newmarket, he was responsible for looking after the four-year-old bay-coloured gelding Fujiyama Crest, a decent enough animal who had won a few races for Mr Hata, his elderly Japanese owner. Back in June the owner had travelled over to England to see the horse run at Royal Ascot, where, partnered by Pat Eddery, it had finished ninth of twenty-six runners over a 2½ mile race, one of the longest contests in the flat racing calendar – but Mr Hata was unable to make it to Ascot for today's meeting.

Today Fujiyama Crest was carrying top weight in the Gordon Carter Handicap – a contest in which he had triumphed twelve months previously. The nation's bookies and newspaper tipsters were not anticipating a repeat performance. In the betting shops' 'Early Bird' lists of odds, chalked up on a daily basis before the betting exchanges at the racecourse got underway much later in the afternoon, he was on offer at generous-looking odds of 12/1 or better. Few racing writers fancied Fujiyama Crest following the disappointment of his last race, the Northumberland Plate on 29 June at Newcastle when he finished far down the field, even though today he was to be ridden by reigning champion jockey Frankie Dettori. Dettori knew the horse quite well, having ridden him three times before – in fact, he had won the same race on him last year, not to mention the race before that at Sandown.

Not surprisingly, Derek Heeney did fancy Fujiyama – and intended to win himself a few bob as a result. 'He'd been humping 10 stone in handicaps earlier in the season,' he recalled, 'and hadn't come to himself before – but he always let you know when he was ready, and I was always confident.' However, Heeney wouldn't have time to place a bet in the local Newmarket betting shop where he was a well known customer, for among Stoute's three runners at Ascot that afternoon was Soviet Line in the big race of the day, the valuable and prestigious Queen Elizabeth II Stakes, in which he had finished third in 1995. Soviet Line did not like being away from home, so, to give him time to settle once he'd arrived at the course, all three horses were travelling to Ascot bright and early. Derek had a 6 a.m. start, thus his Fujiyama flutter was entrusted to his wife.

ANOTHER WOMAN WHO WOKE up with betting on her mind that morning was Pat Epton, a 51-year-old mum working as a cleaner in Lincolnshire. Something of a Frankie Dettori fan who also enjoyed a regular bet, Pat had noticed that Frankie was riding in each of the afternoon's seven races. She reckoned he was the man for the big occasion – and they didn't come much bigger than the opening day of the British Festival of Racing meeting – so this ought to be a good afternoon's sport. To make sure she didn't miss out on any of his anticipated winners, Pat decided to splash out on all seven horses to the tune of 50p a time.

If Pat was a Frankie follower, Darren Yates was a Frankie fanatic. It was not a trait shared by his wife Annaley: that morning she told him in no uncertain terms that his obsession with backing all of Frankie's runners willy-nilly had to cease. Darren's joinery business in Morecambe, Lancashire was not going well, and Annaley felt he shouldn't be frittering away their disposable income gambling on Dettori – indeed, on any jockey for that matter! To keep the peace, Darren agreed that it was a waste of money they could ill afford, but privately he decided to have one more go at backing Frankie's full book of rides at Ascot, and Annaley would remain unaware that £67.58 of their dwindling resources would be at the mercy of the Italian's fortunes. 'He came in every Saturday to place a 50p Super

Heinz, backing certain jockeys to go through the card,' recalled Eddie Gough, the manager of the William Hill branch in Morecambe where Darren was a regular. This time Yates nominated all seven of Frankie's rides and added a £1 each-way accumulator to the usual Super Heinz. Darren had also opted to accept the Early Bird odds available on six of the seven races that guaranteed he would receive those odds, regardless of the eventual Starting Price. By also paying up front the standard nine pence in the pound deductions (to cover betting duty and a levy towards the finances of horse racing), he would avoid any subsequent deductions from his winnings.

Kevin Nightingale, a trainee betting-shop manager for Coral, opened up his Battersea branch with few good thoughts for Frankie Dettori. For obvious reasons betting-shop staff are generally forbidden from placing bets with their own company, so the day before he had visited a William Hill branch nearby to collect a few pounds he had won on the dogs, and reinvest the proceeds on the horses. Not being one to study form, he had opted for an each-way Lucky 31 bet on Frankie Dettori's five runners at Haydock Park. Not one of them had even been placed. 'The following morning, the Saturday,' says Nightingale, 'the first bet I took was a £5 each-way accumulator on his first five runners at Ascot. I was laughing as I told the customer about my bet the day before.'

Fred Done, the eponymous proprietor of a chain of betting shops in the north of England, had called an early morning meeting with his ten area managers. There, during a ten minute chat about the day ahead, he took a fateful decision: to double the bonuses they traditionally offered on all Lucky 15s, Canadians, Super Heinzes and other multiple bets.

In East London Brian Brailey had had a restless night, 'probably about three or four hours sleep, waking and dropping off again'. Therefore, by 8 a.m. he was at his kitchen table with the *Racing Post* and the *Daily Mirror*'s racing pages spread out in front of him. 'Being disabled with epilepsy,' says Brian, 'racing is my one true enjoyment. By about 9.30 I still had not made my selections and I decided to do a Heinz [a complicated 57-bet wager] on Frankie's rides, leaving out Fujiyama Crest. However, by 10 or 10.30 my eyes became very tired and I decided to forget about having a bet.' He tore up his betting slip and chose to have a nap on the sofa instead.

Racing fan Raymond Ion of Newcastle decided that morning to visit his mother, Harriet May, in Freeman Hospital. 'I thought I'd take her home to watch a couple of races on the TV and have a cup of tea,' he says. 'I'd have her back by mid-afternoon.'

For Mary Bolton, Saturday 28 September was her wedding anniversary. A care worker in Glastonbury, Somerset, she helped adults with learning difficulties. That morning she woke up in the Holiday Inn in London's Mayfair where she and her husband John, a farmer and cattle dealer who was forty-nine like her, were enjoying a weekend in the capital to celebrate their nineteenth anniversary. As part of her present, John had given her a bet to place on the Ascot race meeting he would be going to while Mary hit the West End shops. 'We looked at the paper on Friday night,' she remembers, 'and decided on Frankie Dettori, so I said, "Why not all seven?" It was because of his character. He is one of the nice guys in racing, with all his smiling and silly nonsense when he wins.' At Ladbroke's in Dover Street, taking the early-morning odds, they placed a £5 each-way accumulator plus $21 \times £9$ doubles, which, including tax, made a total stake of £216.91.

Albert Sewell has been BBC TV's football statistician for thirty-three years, during which time Desmond Lynam's constant references to his all-encompassing soccer knowledge made him a household name. 'Next to the Great Game, racing is my main sporting interest,' admits Albert. 'On the way to Television Centre that Saturday I called in to William Hill's at Greenford Station for a punt on the day's racing and football. Short of time to study, I just went for Dettori's mounts, breaking them down into a Yankee [on his shorter-priced rides as in the morning papers] and a patent [three singles, three doubles and one treble] on the other three.'

Not many of the daily papers were predicting a bonanza day for Frankie. The *Sun*'s 'Templegate' fancied him to get just one winner, while 'Thunderer' in *The Times* had him down for a blank afternoon. The *Guardian*'s Chris Hawkins, though, was tipping a Fatefully–Fujiyama Crest double. He subsequently explained to me how he'd arrived at his selection. 'I always liked to go for at least one outsider, and I'd been impressed by a regional tipster for a northern evening paper, a man called Donovan, who had won the Top Tipster national competition by following the theory of "biorhythms", based on horses running well during certain cycles and at certain times each season when they came to their best. So I always looked closely at horses contesting races they had won before. Fujiyama Crest had been disappointing last time out but was in good form before that. I was prepared to forgive him that run and thought that although he'd gone up in the weights from the previous year when he'd won the race, the rise was not excessive.'

Meanwhile, over in Surrey, David Ashforth had weighed the priorities rather differently. Ashforth was the top writer for the racing world's bible, the *Sporting Life*, the paper that had chronicled just about every event of any import in the horse racing world since 1859. That morning he considered nipping over to Ascot – until his wife Lesley suggested to him that perhaps he might be better employed mowing the lawn.

HAPPILY, THOUGH, 20,459 RACEGOERS were not so easily deflected from their afternoon's entertainment and headed for the Berkshire track where racing had first taken place in 1711 – at the command of Queen Anne who, out driving from Windsor, decided Ascot Common would make the ideal venue. Nearly 300 years later Ascot was established in the very front rank of Britain's racecourses and as the home of the world-famous Royal meeting. Though not the oldest racecourse (the first recorded race at Newmarket was staged in 1622, and other tracks go back even further), Ascot does possess a genuine sense of history, nicely summed up by Bernard Sculpher, a frequent racegoer who used to live nearby: 'We married in 1968 and rented our first flat as part of an older, rather grand house in a private road almost opposite the racecourse. The road was used by the racehorses and their lads for relaxing before, and cooling off after, racing. Some great names wandered past our front gate. Nothing would give me greater pleasure than to take a walk round part of the course where the road intersects. Just stop and admire the view from the Golden Gates at the far end, back to the Grandstand; it is a truly magnificent sight. On a quiet Sunday morning with no crowds around, it always seemed to me to have an eerie, almost ghost-like quality. You could be forgiven for hearing the faint echo of yesterday's heroes, both equine and human.'

With the arrival of the first punters, the on-course bookmakers were also starting to make their entrance. Gary Wiltshire had got up that morning in his hard-earned, £500,000 house in Buckinghamshire with no intention to be at Ascot at all. He'd been planning to spend his working day at Worcester racecourse. However, before setting off he'd taken another look at the Ascot card. 'I thought,' he remembers of that fatefully impulsive decision, 'that it looked a hard one for punters . . .'.

Stuck in a tailback on the M32, Bristol bookie Andy Smith was trying to get to Ascot where he'd intended to be all along. Eventually, in his frustration, he came to the decision he would later describe as 'my great escape' and – in a mirror image of Wiltshire's about-turn – scrapped his plans to stand at Ascot and headed instead for Worcester.

William Hill's public relations man David Hood left his house in Maidenhead at 11.30 that morning for the twenty-minute drive to Ascot. As he approached his car, he saw it had been broken into and several items had been stolen. 'The splinters of glass on the floor,' he reflected, 'told me the day was already going pear-shaped.'

MEANWHILE, FRANKIE DETTORI HAD begun that Saturday morning on the gallops – riding work – followed by a visit from his physiotherapist Michael Rogers. 'He had been having treatment all week on a niggling injury,' says Mr Rogers. 'On leaving his house I asked him if he thought he would have a good day. After looking in the *Racing Post* he said, "I could have an each-way chance in the first, and I may win the third."' Not bad tipping – as far as it went!

In fact, by that morning Frankie had come to feel a little more optimistic about his prospects than he had the previous evening when he'd arrived home from Haydock having drawn a complete blank. 'I was thinking about riding Mark of Esteem that much that I didn't ride that great at Haydock,' he was to admit later. To his fiancée Catherine, his assessment of his chances at Ascot had been positively pessimistic: 'I remember pacing up and down the kitchen telling her, "I've got a bad feeling about Saturday . . .".' But by the time he had been interviewed over the phone by John Francome on Channel Four's *Morning Line* programme on Saturday morning he was, according to producer Mark Jackson, 'upbeat and bullish'.

Dettori was being driven to the course a couple of hours before racing began by his regular driver, Colin 'Ackers' Rate, a long-time friend who had been with him at Luca Cumani's stables in earlier days. Had any punter been fortunate enough to get a word with the jockey during that journey, he would certainly have wanted to be on Frankie's mount in the Queen Elizabeth II Stakes. 'We travelled to Ascot,' said Frankie later, 'with a single race on our minds.' Dettori's agent Matty Cowing, who had booked his package of rides, was harbouring somewhat more ambitious thoughts. 'I thought Frankie might get four winners,' he would later claim to Helen Johnstone of the *Sunday Telegraph*. When they arrived, Frankie was in a perky mood, good humour having overcome the previous night's doubts, and at the entrance to a course not noted for its sense of humour or informality, he greeted one of Ascot's characteristic 'jobsworths' by cheekily knocking his bowler hat off. Woe betide any run-of-the-mill racegoers attempting such frivolity – they wouldn't have made it further than the entrance gates. 'The Ascot Authority will refuse admission,' warned the racecard, 'to anyone considered to be inappropriately dressed. Shorts, singlets and bare tops are not permitted in the Grandstand.'

For this special afternoon's racing, however, the course had tried hard to soften its austere image. Anxious to persuade a younger clientele to experience a sport traditionally having an older profile, it had pulled out all the promotional stops. Specifically to encourage families to come along, the gates opened at 11.30 a.m., two and a half hours before the first race, so that children could take full advantage of the playground, pony rides, creches, fairground rides, Punch & Judy show, clowns, street performers, Eli the bear, screenings of *The Lion King*, a miniature Legoland from nearby Windsor and a caricature artist in the Grandstand. 'As a keen racing fan,' says Jimmie Yardley of Eltham, 'I am anxious to encourage my son James to share my love of racing.' Perhaps at the age of only seventeen months, as young James was on 28 September 1996, we may doubt that he fully comprehended Burlington Berties and Double-Carpets. Nevertheless, it was this plethora of child-friendly events that enabled Mr Yardley to persuade his wife to accompany him to a day's racing at Ascot – though 'for some unfathomable reason,' he concedes, 'the wife believed that in practice this would mean her looking after James while I concentrated unprofitably on matters equine'.

While at least one racegoer that day hitch-hiked all the way from Paris just to see his hero Frankie Dettori in action (we only know this from a friend of his, who says he's 'too shy to tell the world about it'), Pete Gwilliam, on the other hand, was at Ascot partly in a business capacity. 'Working in finance' at the time, he'd chosen Saturday 28 September for a hospitality event to thank clients for business his company had received during the year. Over lunch they had Channel 4's Derek Thompson talk them – 'hopelessly' – through the card. 'He, like me, failed to pinpoint any of Frankie's winners.'

Thompson, renowned throughout the racing and betting worlds for his genial ubiquity, was clearly a busy man that day, because in addition to working for the Irish broadcaster RTE, he had also agreed to do a number of pre-race talks to some guests of Coral. They were to take place on a stage in front of the Grandstand with Rob Hartnett, a personable, knowledgeable Irishman well-known in racing as a high-profile public relations man for, most recently, the Tote, and at that time frontman for Coral. 'I had risen early to have a good look at the form,' remembers Hartnett, 'so that I would give the impression I knew what I was talking about. My opening line in the previews was to watch out for Frankie – that he was going to have a good day. I thought Wall Street, Mark of Esteem and Lochangel would provide him with a treble and that he was going to be the star at the expense of the bookies. I distinctly remember Tommo laughing at this, commenting on how the bookies never lose and that nobody should feel sorry for them. He was probably right about the second part,' adds Hartnett.

And before the first race got underway, Derek Thompson had a third opportunity to participate in a baffling omen of the forthcoming events. Though Bernard Sculpher was by now living in Reading, Ascot had retained a special significance for him and his wife, and that day they had arrived in plenty of time to have a snack lunch; he recalls 'a strangely quiet atmosphere' in the hours before there were too many people about. After their meal, they heard an announcement stating that before racing began, Frankie Dettori would be interviewed in front of the stands by Derek Thompson; so they went down to listen. 'We were very close to the interview area,' says Mr Sculpher, 'and my wife said she would like to get his autograph on her programme. "What a great idea," I said, and as soon as the interviews were over she wandered down to the platform. A few minutes later she reappeared, beaming from ear to ear. I said, "Did you get it?" "Oh, yes – and what a lovely man he is!" she said, handing me her programme to admire. I stopped dead in my tracks. After a few minutes my wife said, "Are you all right? You seem a little quiet . . .". The great man's autograph was written across the racecard, plain for all to see: "*Derek Thompson*."'

CHAPTER TWO

'HORSES CAN FEEL YOU BLINKING . . . THE DIFFERENCE BETWEEN HAVING A HORSE RELAXED AND HAVING HIM RUN AWAY IS THE EDGE OF A RAZOR BLADE'

FRANKIE DETTORI

OVER THE HUNDREDS OF years during which horse racing has grown and flourished, the sport has generally kept itself to itself. Only on Grand National and Derby day does it transcend its minority appeal as a natural home for the privileged classes, and gatecrash the consciousness of the man or woman in the street. And when it does, it is often the horse rather than the human attracting the limelight – Desert Orchid, Red Rum or Shergar, for example. From time to time a racing personality has established himself or herself (almost invariably him, with only Jenny Pitman ever seriously managing to challenge this bias) on the wider sporting stage, but they have been few and far between. So few and so far that when a recent TV quiz asked the question, 'Which sport features in the weekly Channel 4 programme *Morning Line*?' the answer given was 'Angling'.

In the late nineteenth century, however, champion jockey Fred Archer was the first horse racing personality to become a national celebrity, albeit in an era when the plethora of diversionary entertainment readily available today was non-existent. And it is a strangely coincidental echo down the ages that the date on which Archer rode his first ever winner, two-year-old filly Athol Daisy, in 1870 at the now long-defunct Chesterfield track, was 28 September. Stranger still that throughout the years this date has cropped up again and again to mark significant racing occasions.

As long ago as 1779 on that date, the even-money favourite Tommy won the fourth St Leger – a race which is still around today as the longest surviving Classic. In 1790 George Searle won the Leger for a then record third time, riding Ambidexter. John Singleton junior won the Leger on Orville in 1802 (but was dead within three months). On 28 September 1932 the members' grandstand at Kempton race-course was destroyed by fire. In 1973 Derby-winning jockey Joseph Marshall died in his home town of Brighton. Also on this day Steve Cauthen, the great Anglophile American who became a champion here, and a role model for Frankie, rode the final winner of the final day of flat racing at Wolverhampton.

On 28 September 1996 Frankie Dettori arrived at Ascot as the reigning champion jockey – albeit unlikely to hang on to the title he had first won in 1994 and retained in 1995. But that morning it was still arguable whether Frankie or his illustrious father, thirteen times Italian champion jockey Gianfranco Dettori, could boast the more outstanding riding record. By the late afternoon there was no argument whatsoever.

IN MY JOB AS Media Relations Director for bookmakers William Hill I have also somehow managed to acquire responsibility for dealing with what are loosely termed as Off-Beat Bets – in other words, those for which no one else within the company is prepared to take responsibility. The chances of the Loch Ness Monster turning up in a flying saucer piloted by Elvis Presley, for example – and, believe it or not, I did once accept a bet to that effect, offering odds of 14,000,000/1. They were accepted by London postman Ross McLachan to the tune of 50 pence. He is still confident of being paid out one day.

More commonly, though, I am confronted with requests to lay bets that people's children will grow up to achieve sporting glory. The standard offer is 10,000/1 on a newborn baby or a toddler playing football for England, winning Wimbledon or the Open Championship. Or maybe having a number one hit single, or perhaps even becoming Prime Minister; after all, a few years back a cabbie in Sedgefield got 250/1 about the then newly-elected MP Tony Blair becoming Premier. The odds quoted can be influenced a little by parental connections, but not by a great deal – after all, for every Stella McCartney, Liam Botham or Jamie Redknapp, there are any number of Sean Lennons, James Majors, Mark Thatchers and Zowie Bowies.

Racing has always been an incestuous business – you could lose yourself trying to track Lester Piggott's family tree back through top-class racing tribes like the Cannons, Days, Rickabys and Armstrongs, while Henry Cecil's stepfather was trainer Sir Cecil Boyd-Rochfort and he in turn wed Julie, the daughter of the Classic-winning trainer Sir Noel Murless. Nevertheless, I can only surmise what price Gianfranco Dettori could have got on his son Lanfranco following in his hoof-prints. With hindsight, even 50–1 would have been too generous.

Gianfranco himself was born the son of a bricklayer on 25 April 1941, and, besides becoming champion jockey thirteen times in Italy, he also rode successive 2000 Guineas winners in England (both for Henry Cecil – in 1975 on Bolkonski and in 1976 on Wollow). His son Lanfranco was born on 15 December 1970. When he was just six months old Frankie's parents split up, and the young boy was to live with his mother Iris Maria, once a circus trapeze artist, until he was five, before moving in with his father and stepmother.

Football was Frankie's early sporting passion, and it is noteworthy that he recalls being 'forced' to ride for the first time at the age of six. Within a couple of years, though, his father had bought him a pony called Sylvia, on which he would contest his first race at the age of nine – a Pony Derby at the San Siro racecourse. Frankie's career did not get off to a winning start – he was unseated straight into a water jump. At the age of eleven Frankie began punting when he went racing: 'This was when I really got the love of horse racing.' This is an extremely interesting comment made by Frankie in the nearest thing to an autobiography yet published about him, *A Year In The Life of Frankie Dettori*. It suggests that he has a strong feel for betting himself and is therefore fully aware of the importance of the relationship between racing and gambling, and appreciates just what a victory means to the punters who have backed him.

Jockeys, of course, are officially prohibited from placing bets, although this is a rule which in practical terms is entirely impossible to police. As recently retired former top jump jockey Graham Bradley, a man who was suspended for two months for having a modest £50 wager, observed, 'If every jockey who's had a bet at some time owned up to his crime then there wouldn't be enough riders to take part in an average handicap hurdle.'

Frankie became a stable lad at the highly thought of d'Allessio yard, where for fifteen years his father had been first jockey – to trainer Sergio Cumani, father of Luca, himself a very successful trainer in England. Any thoughts that this would be a fast-track route to the top of racing must have been tempered by his father's caution-ary advice: 'Only one in a thousand makes it as a jockey.' Gianfranco arranged for his son to spend six months with Luca Cumani (a man whose stated opinion it is that 'nobody is born a jockey') at his Newmarket stables, followed by a further six months with Patrick Biancone in Chantilly before returning to Italy.

Frankie arrived in England aged just fourteen and having trav-elled against his will to fulfil his father's arrangement with Cumani. 'When he sent me to England he gave me a million lire. At the time it was worth £366. He told me there was no more where that came from. I didn't learn English, I just picked it up as I went along. I think the first word I ever learned was goodbye.' Frankie also harboured a bizarre early ambition: 'I was intent on becoming a petrol pump atten-dant. I know it seems funny, but the price of petrol was very high, and it seemed the right job to be in.' Being cruel to be kind proved to be an inspired tactic by Dettori senior. The Cumani experiment proved so successful that parts two and three of the masterplan would never have to be put into action. Having ridden his first winner in Turin in November 1986, Frankie got off the mark in England on Lizzie Hare at Goodwood on 9 June 1987.

His first actual ride in England at Kempton over Easter 1987 had seen him finish second on Peter Walwyn's Mustakbil. After the race, Frankie had the nerve to tell Walwyn, known as Basil Fawlty for his occasional irascibility, in his heavily accented English that his horse was 'fet', which Walwyn soon realized translated as 'fat'. Apoplectic at the insult, Walwyn called him a 'cheeky little blighter', or 'bugger', depending on which report you choose to believe! He also promptly banned Dettori from riding for him for a year, although it should be recorded that the horse never did win a race.

In 1989 Frankie became champion apprentice – the first teenaged champ to ride over 100 winners in a season since a certain L. Piggott, with whom Frankie would later team up during the 'Long Fellow's' short-lived career as a trainer. Punters had already noted the new kid on the block for his eye-catching, all-action style and his lively, outgoing personality. All too frequently, though, successful apprentices fail to fulfil their potential once they lose the weight allowance to which they are entitled at that stage. In 1990 Frankie became Cumani's first choice jockey, although the arrangement stopped short of including a financial retainer to make him stable jockey. In 1991 he won his first Derby, the German version, on Temporal.

The first setback in the young Italian's rise to prominence came in 1993 when it was revealed that he had been cautioned by police who had found drugs on him. This incident subsequently led to the Hong Kong authorities revoking the offer that had been made to him to ride there for a year, an intended career move which had not played well with his mentor. The trainer took some while to forgive and forget, believing that such a move would do his career little good. At this point Frankie was being publicly criticized for the first time, and later confessed, 'I was at my lowest ebb.' Advice from controversial trainer/owner/punter Barney Curley was to refocus Frankie's mind and set him back on the right track: 'He made me understand that I had too much, too early in my life.'

On 17 April 1993 he rode his first four-timer, landing odds of 15,969/1 at Newbury, on Linpac West at 25/1; Inchinor at 7/2; the Queen's horse, Tissisisat 20/1; and Winged Victory at 11/2. By 1994 Frankie had become stable jockey to Newmarket's John Gosden, who trained a powerful string for Sheikh Mohammed. Having finished runner-up in the jockey title race in 1993 behind Pat Eddery, with 149 winners to his credit, Frankie hatched a cunning plan to 'steal' the title in 1994 by riding at the winter all-weather meetings, which were generally boycotted by the more established riders who took the opportunity of a holiday to prepare for the rigours of the turf season to come. So successful was this ploy that by the start of the turf section of the season, Frankie had already chalked up over fifty winners – a virtually insuperable lead. He finished the season as champion with 233 winners to his credit, satisfyingly four ahead of another great champion's record seasonal score – his dad's. During this season Frankie's partnership with hugely popular sprinter Lochsong increased his public profile. He also went to Churchill Downs, Kentucky and won the prestigious Breeders Cup Mile race (worth $500,000 in prize money) on Luca Cumani-trained Barathea. He celebrated with his new trademark flying dismount, a move borrowed from Frankie's hero, flamboyant South American jockey Angel Cordero, who rode over 7,200 winners in the States before retiring in May 1992, having suffered multiple injuries in a horrendous fall at Aqueduct in January of that year. Not everyone was impressed with this innovation; notably one Mr D. Baker of London even went to the lengths of writing to the *Racing Post*, complaining about 'Dettori's yobbish, self-congratulatory antics', which 'marred my pleasure at Barathea's win'. Frankie's old friend Peter Walwyn supported this view: 'I do wish he would desist from his ridiculous habit of throwing himself off a winning horse at a big meeting. It is completely unnecessary and could easily scare a horse, to say nothing of the risk of breaking an ankle. I feel that such behaviour should be prohibited officially.'

Frankie retained his title in 1995 with 216 winners (variously recorded as 211 in the *BBC Radio 5 Live Yearbook* and 217 in Frankie's own *A Year In the Life*) and after a lengthy battle with Jason Weaver, who had also got wise to the all-weather tactic and copied it himself. Classic Cliché won the 1995 St Leger, giving Dettori his 1000th winner in England.

As the 1996 season began, Frankie was confident that he could complete a hat trick of titles. He was backed by the John Gosden stable and Sheikh Mohammed's Godolphin set-up, which consisted of the 'Boss' himself, his racing manager Simon Crisford, trainer Saeed bin Suroor and assistant Tom Albertrani – oh, and the odd extremely good horse or two. The brainchild of the Maktoum Family, the ruling family of Dubai, and above all HH Sheikh Mohammed bin Rashid Al Maktoum, Godolphin was established in 1994, with the intention of breaking away from the tried and tested methods of training horses for the European Flat season. Dubai itself was an ideal location from which to send runners to Hong Kong, Singapore, Japan, Australia, Europe and America. Each winter a select team of horses is brought to Dubai's Al Quoz Stables, the clement weather from October to April allowing the advantage of uninterrupted training schedules, before being moved to the European base at Moulton Paddocks in Newmarket for the summer racing season. The formula has proved so successful that Godolphin is already recognized as one of the most powerful stables in the world, aspiring to win the very top races, from America's Triple Crown to the Japan Cup.

But the year of 1996 began under a cloud, with Frankie still mourning the tragic death of Barney Curley's son Chuck, killed in a car crash in Newmarket. This year, too, the championship would be calculated on winning rides between March and November, excluding all-weather winners outside of that time frame. However, Frankie did ride nine early all-weather winners just to keep his hand in.

In May Frankie emulated his father by winning the 2000 Guineas on Mark of Esteem for Godolphin, getting the better of Even Top ridden by Philip Robinson, who thought he had won it in a photo finish. The race had a couple of odd sequels – Frankie was fined £500 for jumping off his horse before entering the unsaddling enclosure, while he, Robinson and third-placed Jason Weaver (Bijou d'Inde) were found guilty of excessive use of the whip and suspended for eight, four and two days respectively. 'I was banned for trying too hard,' complained Frankie.

In June he finished third in the Derby on 25/1 outsider Shantou – on whom he would subsequently win the St Leger for Sheikh Mohammed and trainer John Gosden, who had been coming in for some recent media criticism of his big race record – and was runner-up in The Oaks on Pricket. Then on 12 June he set a personal record by riding three winners at both Yarmouth and Kempton, one of his six being a certain Fatefully. That day's work was memorable for Frankie for another reason – it was the closest he had come to matching his father Gianfranco's wonderful display back in 1982 when he had ridden six consecutive winners at Milan, only to be short-headed on the seventh.

But the very next day Frankie broke his elbow in a fall in the Newbury paddock when grey filly Shawwani reared up and went over on to her back with the jockey still on board. He didn't return to action until 9 August, although the injury did not prevent him from turning up at Royal Ascot, resplendent in morning suit (borrowed from jockey Bruce Raymond), top hat, flamboyant, multicoloured tie, red rose buttonhole – and his arm in a sling. Then he came back and won the Goodwood Tripleprint Celebration Mile on Mark of Esteem. However, he received a four-day ban from the stewards, who took exception to his and Pat Eddery's use of the whip as they battled out the finish of the St Leger.

After Fred Archer, Sir Gordon Richards was the next great racing figure, riding 4,870 winners between 1921 and 1954, and dominating the title race year in, year out, giving best just three times between 1925 and 1953. Lester Piggott inherited the mantle of 'housewives' choice' in the big races, displaying his uncanny ability in the saddle by booting home major winners, heavily supported by public money time after time to the despair of bookmakers nationwide. Piggott was champion jockey eleven times, but it was his knack of manoeuvring himself onto the best horse on Derby day and in other Classic races in particular that really struck a chord with punters everywhere. He triumphed at Epsom in the Blue Riband event a record nine times, winning twenty-one other Classics. Lester totalled 4,493 flat victories in Britain, plus twenty more over hurdles. Dettori has had just one public ride over hurdles – 'I was absolutely terrified' – but decided it is an art best practised by specialists: 'They must be mad.' Lester's popularity was almost exclusively attributable to his performances on board a horse. A less than communicative character when standing on his own two feet, he was difficult to warm to on a human level.

So perhaps Frankie's success, achieved (at the time of writing) despite the lack of an Epsom Derby win, is understandable in the context of an era in which the 'Sport of Kings' itself at long last woke up to the necessity of selling itself to a wider – and younger – market. It has introduced a more commercial outlook in order to guarantee a healthy future that other sports which have cashed in on the opportunities afforded by satellite TV and a personality obsessed media have engendered.

ANYONE WISHING TO BET on all seven of Frankie's runners that late September morning in 1996 could happily have done so at a variety of odds with different bookmakers. These were the odds on offer at William Hill's branches and with its telephone betting operation:

Wall Street – 11/4
Diffident – 10/1
Mark of Esteem – 5/2
Decorated Hero – 10/1
Fatefully – 9/2
Fujiyama Crest – 11/1

There were no 'Early Bird' odds, as these prices are generally known, for Lochangel's race.

TAKING AN ACCUMULATOR BET on all six of these horses – a bet which would only pay out in the event that every selection was successful – would have produced winning odds of 104,815.25/1. In other words, for a stake of just £1, the winning punter would pocket a return of £104,815.25 – plus their £1 stake money back. So, rather than the now-immortalized 25,095/1 (the cumulative odds of Frankie's seven timer based on the official starting prices – although even this figure is half a point too short), the true winning odds can only be calculated as the Early Bird odds for the six races quoted, together with the starting price of Lochangel, 5/4, which comes to 235,834.31/1 – almost a quarter of a million to one!

The potential advantage for the gambler in the Early Bird odds was the certainty of having taken guaranteed odds about each horse that could not be changed by subsequent events. The downside, however, was that the odds available in the afternoon could possibly be larger than those accepted in the morning – indeed, in two of the races this would turn out to be the case. The advantage for the bookmaker was that punters were enticed to put their bets on early in the day, before, perhaps, being fully aware of the going or jockey changes. The massive potential disadvantage to them – which few took seriously – was that they were acquiring potential liabilities about which they could do little and might even be unaware of until it was too late to react.

Betting in this country is organized on the principle of 'the tail wagging the dog'. The odds at which bets struck in the betting shops are settled are determined by the bets struck at the racecourse. Even a race meeting at which the total attendance is in the hundreds, therefore, will be determining just what odds are applied to the bets placed by hundreds of thousands of off-course customers in the licensed betting offices. As Tony Stafford, the *Daily Telegraph*'s respected racing specialist, puts it: 'In a way, the bookmaker is hostage to the betting ring, but naturally the professionals in the ring are aware that they need to be as prudent as they can, without causing punters to withdraw their patronage.'

This may seem somewhat illogical. From a bookie's point of view, heavily-backed 'popular' horses in the shops can start at artificially or unfairly long odds if, for some reason, that support is not mirrored at the racecourse. But it is a system that has stood the test of time and which the great majority of punters are happy to see continue. Bookmakers occasionally suggest half-heartedly that a computerized system be introduced taking into account how much money has been bet in the shops and at least used for settling the bets struck there. Deeply suspicious betting-shop patrons and their public champions like John McCririck – a self-confessed failed bookmaker himself – resist such proposals vigorously, fearing that bets calculated in this manner could be susceptible to manipulation not to their advantage. (Such anti-bookmaker scepticism does not seem to preclude accepting the odd lucrative earner to perform official opening ceremonies for the larger bookmaking chains' new shops.) But it is important at this point, in view of the controversy that raged within the bookmaking industry following the Magnificent Seven, to take a look at how well alternative ways of making odds have worked, and what the consequences can be of sticking with the traditional system.

In February 2001, as domestic horse racing was shut down to help limit the spread of foot and mouth disease, betting shops were provided with live coverage of racing from Dubai's Nad Al Sheba course, where no bookmakers or betting of any kind are permitted. In order to enable punters to bet, therefore, bookmakers created their own odds, and Satellite Information Services, which were co-ordinating the television transmissions, developed a way of supplying a 'Starting Price' system. 'A selection of bookmakers which will include independents, the Big 3 (Coral, Hill, Ladbrokes), the Tote and Stanley, will send prices into SIS,' explained Brent Dolan, Racing Information Controller at SIS, 'and I will co-ordinate a first show transmission through our text system around ten minutes before the scheduled "off". If there are changes, we will try to transmit them perhaps five minutes before the off, and maybe as they go behind the stalls.' The SPs were determined by Bill Hooker, senior SP returner for the Press Association, assisted by an SIS racecourse representative. This system was duly implemented and, I understand, no protest riots broke out in the nation's betting shops, although the *Racing Post* predictably managed to infer problems by suggesting that 'bookmakers and SIS moved to allay fears about the prices being returned on racing in Dubai'. The SP Executive Chairman, David Oldrey, had no fears needing to be allayed. He commented, 'In the interests of making life go on as normal in the betting shops while the foot and mouth crisis continues, it was felt this was a worthwhile measure to take.'

One perfectly legal, accepted way in which bookmakers are able to influence the odds on offer at a race meeting is to have a representative on hand there who can place bets with the on-course bookmakers in order to change the odds on a horse for which the off-course bookmaker is carrying a large liability. If, for example, three very well fancied horses have won the first three races of the afternoon, the off-course bookmakers might well discover that in the fourth race many customers have bet on the same horse, to complete their accumulative bets, such as yankees. It is now to the bookmakers' considerable advantage that the fourth horse starts at the shortest odds possible. To try and bring that about, they will place enough money with as many bookmakers as necessary to ensure that the price of that horse is significantly shortened. The weight of money bet at the course thus reflects the weight of money bet in the off-course outlets. Punters do not like this practice, but have to accept that, as the price of the heavily-backed runner shortens, so the prices of the other runners lengthen, thus making them better value for the punters who have bet on them. Never would the efficacy of this system come under greater examination from the diametrically-opposed desires of the different practitioners of the bookmaking art than during the afternoon on which Frankie Dettori urged home winner after winner.

IF WE NOW TURN to the racing itself, discovering the monetary value of a horse race is not quite as straightforward as it might appear. The first race on the card that September afternoon at Ascot – scheduled off time, 2.00 p.m. – was the Cumberland Lodge Stakes, a Group Three race run over a distance of 1½ miles. Frankie Dettori was on board a chestnut colt called Wall Street, drawn in the number seven stall. A three-year-old, it had been bred in America and was carrying a weight of 8st. 6lbs. Owned by Godolphin, it had been trained by Saeed bin Suroor.

The Ascot racecard explained that the 'estimated total value' of the Cumberland Lodge Stakes was £54,000, and that there was £50,000 'added to stakes'. A helpful chap at Weatherby's (racing's bureaucrats and administrators) explained this to me: 'The £50,000 is the initial prize fund. Entry fees [paid for all intended runners] are added in to get the Estimated Total Value – although that should be accurately known when the racecard is compiled.' With me so far?

Next on the racecard we see 'Penalty Value' – £31,400 – which is the amount of money credited to winning connections before deductions are made to cover the fees payable to the trainer, jockey and stable staff. The Penalty Value is also subsequently used to determine whether the winner will be allocated additional weight in future races. And then there is 'Owners' prize money' – £24,592 – that's the amount due after the other deductions are made. Then we have the self-explanatory Second Prize of £10,170, Third of £5,058, and Fourth of £2,442 – paid to the owners of those placed horses.

There is a further confusing factor in as much as some races boast an actual trophy. The value of that trophy is subtracted from the prize money on offer, but it can usually be reinstated if the owner decides to forgo the bauble. For each race on this Ascot card there was also £100 on offer to the lad or girl responsible for the 'best turned-out' runner, and £100 to the lad or girl responsible for the winner. These amounts are additional to the race's total prize money.

The pinnacle of the sport is the Group One races – Classic races and other races of major international importance. The Group Two category is just below championship standard; Group Three races, like this first race at Ascot, the Cumberland Lodge Stakes, are those of mainly domestic importance within the European sequence of 'Pattern' races.

RACEGOERS LIKED THE LOOK of Wall Street's chances, even though it had yet to run over the race's distance; the horse was backed from longest odds of 5/2 down to 7/4, before settling at 2/1 favourite, courtesy of one bet of £6,750 to a stake of £3,000. (The first figure represents the potential winnings, the second the figure gambled – add the two together for the total return.) There were also two £2,000 bets, one at 5/2, the other at 2/1; a couple of £1,000 bets; and three of £800. The field came under orders bang on time.

Although Wall Street had previously won at Newbury when coming off a very strong pace, this time Frankie decided to show faith in his mount's stamina. 'Frankie is setting out to make all by the look of it,' observed Peter O'Sullevan very early on in his race commentary. By taking the initiative, Frankie was inviting the other six runners to catch him if they could.

The third favourite in the race at 4/1 was Salmon Ladder, trained by Paul Cole, a horse that held a special place in the affections of its rider Richard Quinn. Earlier in the year their win together at Hamilton had enabled Quinn to complete the notable feat of riding a winner on every flat racecourse in Britain. Now Quinn drove the four-year-old along to join battle with Wall Street, and with 2 furlongs remaining had every chance. However, as they swung into the straight, Frankie had taken a little peep at his main rival. Holding a little in reserve as a result, he rode out Wall Street to come home half a length to the good.

The combination came in to the winners' enclosure to a low-key reception with polite, yet somewhat restrained applause. 'That wasn't the plan,' explained Godolphin's Racing Manager, Simon Crisford, on Wall Street's making the running, 'but we were confident he would stay well.' Dettori later commented, 'This was one of my best chances of the afternoon. I had a good feeling about the race, which I was able to dominate.' The BBC's Julian Wilson noted something else: 'Royal Court was the first horse beaten – the ring knew something.' He was pointing out how little betting support this horse had attracted, despite very sound form, and its odds had drifted to 11/4. This often points to a horse that will fail to run up to its best form. His fellow BBC summariser, the former jockey Jimmy Lindley, agreed with him that 'Frankie Dettori had no doubts he would get the mile and a half. I thought Salmon Ladder might wear him down.' It was Frankie's 82nd winner of the season.

The talking point after the race, though, was not Frankie Dettori at all, but rather the severe ride given to his mount by Richard Quinn, who reportedly 'hit Salmon Ladder nine times, several times above shoulder height and very severely'. *Raceform* declared sternly that it was 'about time the British Horseracing Board sorted out the whole whip problem once and for all, before British racing becomes the laughing stock of the world' – even though the Ascot Stewards' Secretary, William Nunneley, subsequently maintained that during the whole day's racing, 'we never had to look at any one particular incident for the whip'.

THERE WAS AN INTRIGUING technical aspect of this first race.

In the early days of horse racing, one owner would pit his best horse against that of a rival racehorse owner. They would arrange to race over an agreed distance for an agreed stake – perhaps 1000 guineas. In effect, both owners, in accepting these 'winner take all' conditions, were taking on a 1000 guinea bet at odds of 'even money'. Whichever owner's horse won would make a profit of 1000 guineas: this was also the amount he stood to lose. Fine as it stood, but this type of betting was impossible to widen out, and prevented interested observers and spectators from becoming involved by betting on their own fancy. Eventually, therefore, a few shrewd characters realized that if they were to offer odds about the contestants in a race, whilst incorporating a percentage of profit margin into those odds to enable them to make it pay, anyone who wished to enjoy a flutter – small or large – could be accommodated.

For example, on the two-horse race in which each had a theoretical equal, or even-money, chance, the bookmaker could offer one of the runners at the true 'even money' odds – the equivalent of 50 per cent in betting percentage terms – and the other at, say, 4/5 – or 55.56 per cent. Now, if the bookmaker accepted bets of £10 for each runner, he would break even if the even-money shot won the race but he would make a £2 profit if the 4/5 chance was successful, as the backer would receive an £8 profit on his £10 stake money. In percentage terms the bookmaker would be making a book of 50 per cent plus 55.56 per cent, giving him a theoretical profit of 5.6% in a hypothetical ideal world.

The downside of this system is that there is nothing to prevent the two punters, who in our first example staked £10 each on the two different runners, from both deciding to back the same one. In that case the bookie would be left in a highly undesirable situation whereby one result would mean all his bets were winning ones, and the other would mean they were all losers. To try to guard against this, the bookmaker would then amend his odds in an effort to encourage people to back the unfancied runner. So, let's say the punters had plunged on the 4/5 chance, ignoring the even-money shot. The bookie might then decide to make the 4/5 chance less attractive by shortening the odds to 4/7 and to enhance the other runner by lengthening the odds from even-money to, say, 11/8. He would then be betting to a percentage of 63.64 per cent (4/7), plus 42.11 per cent (11/8), which equals 105.75 per cent, still just over 5 per cent in his favour, but enabling him to direct the punters towards the one he wants to lay – in this example, the outsider. By maintaining this theoretical profit percentage – known as the over-round – the odds can be adjusted no matter how many runners contest an event to ensure that, in an ideal world, the bookies' potential liability on the ultimate winner would never exceed the total stake money collected in. If the over-round becomes an under-round, this desirable situation (at least as far as the bookie is concerned) is jeopardised.

Now, you will seldom find a bookie offering odds against both runners in a two-horse race – e.g. 11/10 and 5/4 – because if you calculate the percentages you will find that they add up to 47.62 per cent, plus 44.44 per cent, which equals 92.06 per cent. So, for £92.06 outlay, the punters could back both runners to win a return of £100. That way lies disaster and bankruptcy for the bookie and is why you will never see an individual bookmaker letting that situation occur. But it can happen when a number of bookmakers are betting on the same event but have different opinions. In a tennis match, for example, one bookie could make Henman 4/6 to beat Rusedski, whom he offers at 11/10, while another could take a different view and offer 4/7 Rusedski with Henman at 5/4. Both bookies are now safe within their own percentages, but by backing the two outsiders with each bookie, the punter can in effect make a book of his own in which he cannot lose.

In the betting on the Cumberland Lodge Stakes, the betting 'over-round' in favour of the bookmakers was just 8.8 per cent. What this means is that, if all the money staked on the race were divided out equally in terms of potential liabilities for each runner, in theory the bookmakers would have a percentage profit margin of 8.8 per cent. This is particularly low, meaning that generous odds were on offer, that would be substantially exceeded on the following races.

Perhaps on this high-profile afternoon, at the start of the day when things hadn't really warmed up, the bookies were trying to tempt the punters into action.

Wall Street, though, was given 'a lovely ride', paying a win dividend of £2.70 for £1 on the tote and £1.70 for a place-only bet. Anyone with a £1 accumulator at Starting Price odds on Frankie's mounts now had a total of £3 running on to the next race.

'When Wall Street won I was delighted,' remembers Rob Hartnett, at that time Coral's PR man. 'I had backed him myself and given him to the guests in our box, so everyone was happy.' Did the name of that first winner offer, in the mind of any bookmaker anywhere in the land, even the faintest hint of what was to come? If so, I failed to find him or her during the research for this book. Did no one automatically append the word 'Crash', and then consider briefly if this might be an early omen of disaster?

WALL STREET: First foal of Wajd, a useful middle distance filly who was trained by Andre Fabre; by Northern Dancer. His father, or sire, was Mr Prospector.

RESULT: 1. Wall Street (Dettori) 2/1f. 2. Salmon Ladder (T. Quinn) 4/1. 3. Priolina (J. Quinn) 25/1. 7 ran. Winning distances: ½ length; 4 lengths. Trainer: S. bin Suroor. Tote win return: £2.70.

CHAPTER THREE

'LUCAYAN PRINCE WAS WITHOUT A SHADOW OF DOUBT THE HARD
LUCK STORY OF THE DAY'

RACEFORM ON LUCAYAN PRINCE, 15/8 BEATEN FAVOURITE FOR THE SECOND RACE

TO SET A NEW standard of achievement you must eclipse
everything that has gone before. While we are waiting for the
runners to come out for the second race, therefore, let us survey
the feats of jockeyship that represented the pinnacle of performance prior to Frankie's arrival at the gates of Ascot
racecourse that Saturday morning.

The first post-war jockey to go 'through the card' was Alexander
John Russell, known as Alec or A.J., who rode his first winner in 1935
at Le Tremblay in France, where he had been apprenticed. In 1948 he
came back to Britain after war service in Burma to ply his trade round
the northern tracks.

On Friday 19 July 1957 at the now-closed Bogside racecourse
fourteen miles from Ayr, which used to host the Scottish Grand
National, Alec Russell had mounts in all six races, for six different
trainers. The 2/5 favourite Double Up (trained by Colonel Wilfred
Lyde) opened proceedings for him successfully in the Middleton
Maiden Stakes for two-year-old fillies, and the 2/1 favourite Cligarry
(Harry Blackshaw) then won the Montgreenan Selling Handicap. But
Alec's third victory was somewhat unexpected – the 100/8 chance
Wage Claim (Edward G. Duffy) in the Borland Handicap – as was his
fourth race 8/1 outsider of three, Courtlier (W. Hide), the Fairlie
Handicap. Newton, from the George Boyd yard, easily the most suc-
cessful at the course, was the 8/13 winner of the fifth race, and his
mount in the sixth, Roselime, 11/8 favourite (Ernest Carr) won the
Ardeer handicap by two lengths to complete a 1,132/1 six-timer.

The story was front-page news at the time but it made Russell neither a rich man nor a great celebrity – in fact, as *Cope's Racegoers Encyclopaedia* for the following year pointed out, the jockey was 'still not well known in the south'. Bogside wasn't even Alec's favourite track – that honour went to Lanark (now also closed) where, as is seldom recalled, he had ridden the last winner on the day before his six-in-a-row. Russell rode on until 1973 when an injury forced him out of the game, and died in 1990 at the age of either seventy-one or seventy-three (vanity apparently prompted a certain vagueness about his true date of birth).

Lester Piggott's CV failed to include a through-the-card performance. Among his best multiple achievements were five out of seven at Yarmouth in September 1981, and four out of four for trainer Vincent O'Brien at the Curragh in Ireland in October 1990. The next British jockey to ride six winners on one card in one day was Willie Carson, who did it from seven rides – his other horse was unplaced in the third race – at Newcastle in June 1990, a mere six years before Frankie. Nevertheless, Willie's 3,266/1 accumulator didn't even warrant a mention in 'racing's supreme book of information and statistics', *Ruff's Guide*'s 1990 review of the year, or even in Carson's own autobiography *Up Front* that he wrote with Brough Scott. (Although subsequently, when discussing another occasion on which he rode eight winners out of nine races at Madras in India, the Scot did acknowledge his Newcastle six as 'obviously a great feat which I'll never forget'.)

Willie began that day in 1990 by winning on Arousal, trained by Major Dick Hern, the even-money favourite in a four-horse race, and followed up with Soweto (Gavin Pritchard Gordon), 5/2 favourite in a two-year-old claimer with nine runners. But then he was only sixth in the next on 9/1 shot Parliament Piece. (Recently Carson told me he had been 'looking after' Parliament Piece, but he was possibly only half-joking when he added, 'If his had been the last race, he'd have won.') He came back to win the fourth, the prestigious Northumberland Plate, on trainer Alec Stewart's 9/2 chance Al Maheb; then beat a field of ten on

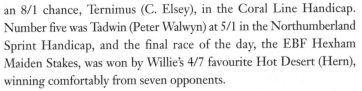

an 8/1 chance, Ternimus (C. Elsey), in the Coral Line Handicap. Number five was Tadwin (Peter Walwyn) at 5/1 in the Northumberland Sprint Handicap, and the final race of the day, the EBF Hexham Maiden Stakes, was won by Willie's 4/7 favourite Hot Desert (Hern), winning comfortably from seven opponents.

It is odd how few people seem to recall Willie's sextet today. I spoke to long serving *Newcastle Journal* sportswriter Doug Moscrop who covered that day for his paper. It was certainly a big deal locally, Doug reckons: 'The Geordies loved Willie and the six-timer did make an impact at the time, but it certainly didn't register like Dettori day. But then, anything that happens north of the Trent struggles for coverage in the nationals . . .'. Another keen follower of racing present that afternoon told me the weather had deteriorated into heavy rain by the time of the final race, which made Willie's reception, therefore, somewhat low key, with the few intrepid fans who welcomed him into the winners' enclosure absolutely soaked to the skin.

But Willie's run of success was actually even more spectacular, for he had also ridden the final winner at Goodwood the evening before – so the six at Newcastle made seven out of eight. Then, on Sunday, he went to The Curragh in Ireland and rode two more consecutive winners – including the small matter of the Irish Derby on Salsabil: nine from ten. His other Curragh mount was a loser, so that was now nine from eleven. But on Monday Carson was still in irresistible form, winning the first three winners of the day at Wolverhampton. Twelve winners from fourteen races.

Going back over these half-forgotten details with me, Willie became justifiably proud of the statistics involved – particularly as they included a Classic and the Newcastle race known as the 'Pitmens' Derby'. Willie also pointed out that on the Saturday at Newcastle, 'Mark Birch's breeches rode all seven winners – my gear had gone missing en route to Newcastle, and Mark kindly loaned me his spare set, in which I won six of the races – and he rode the other winner, Yearsley, wearing his own!' To mark his superb day, Newcastle racecourse gave Willie a free holiday – which he never took up – and a silver plate. As he won race after race, he also received a string of tankards, most of which he subsequently donated to charity.

IF WE GO BACK to racing's early days, a full 123 years before Willie Carson's feat, in June 1867 the fourteen-times champion jockey George Fordham had also booted home six from seven at the long-lost Stockbridge course. (In his other race he actually dead-heated, only to lose out in the subsequent run-off, the accepted way in those days of deciding the outcome.) The legendary Fred Archer, the first superstar jockey and champion for fourteen years from 1874–86, managed this feat twice – at Newmarket in April 1877 and at Lewes in August 1882.

But most prodigious of all was the achievement of twenty-nine-year-old Gordon Richards in October 1933. That day Gordon – later Sir – had ridden all six winners at Chepstow, on the way to what became the staggering sequence of twelve consecutive winners.

HIS MAGNIFICENT DOZEN – AS, interestingly enough, it was dubbed at the time – began on October 3 when he won the last race at Nottingham on Barnby. The next day at Chepstow, Gordon, who would win his seventh of a scarcely credible twenty-six championships that season with 259 winners, kicked off by winning the St Andrews Plate on Manner, the 4/6 favourite. The Clearwell Selling Plate saw a routine win for even-money shot Brush Past, he won the Bulwark Selling Plate on Miss B, and the Severn Stakes on Arcona. Then a five-length cruise for Red Horizon, 7/4 favourite in the Glanely Handicap, set up the perfect six-timer for the filly Delicia to win the Castleford Handicap by a length. On a day when, 'I thought I would only win one race', Richards had gone through the card without ever brandishing his whip in anger. That morning he had even dissuaded the assistant trainer Herbert Arnold, who had taken the train to Chepstow with him, from backing his six mounts in mixed doubles! Richards later learned that Arnold's boss, the Classic-winning trainer Frank Hartigan, 'had a £5 accumulator on me and won several hundred pounds'. For Richards the afternoon was 'a wonderful experience. I had promised to attend a boxing match at Swindon that night,' he recalled, 'and when I turned up they gave me a tremendous reception.'

So, back to Chepstow the next day, where he opened up on The Covenanter at evens, then landed his ninth consecutive winner on Kirrimuir at 4/6, and the tenth with June Rose (9/4). At this point, recorded Richards in his autobiography *My Story*, 'even the book-makers' satchels were being thrown in the air in the general enthusiasm and excitement'. (Bookies must have changed over the years – I reckon it's more likely they were being shaken about to try and find some small change hidden in there to help with the payouts!) In went Montrose at 4/7 – owned, like all the others thus far that day except for June Rose, by Lord Woolavington – and then Lady Swift completed the dozen at even-money.

Would it be unlucky thirteen? The bookies feared not and made Eagle Ray 1/3 favourite, a horse of which Richards said, 'I did not think I could possibly be beaten, as in my view this was the best bet of the whole meeting.' But his luck finally came to an end, and Eagle Ray could only manage third behind fifteen-year-old Doug Smith on the winner, Lament. 'I had the most collywobbles in my stomach,' Smith later remarked, 'when I realized I had beaten Gordon and stopped his run.' The racegoers weren't best pleased by the result, either, and after the last race, taking the bus to Wantage to catch his train home, he heard a fellow passenger mutter darkly, 'If I could lay my hands on the little blighter who beat Gordon today I'd kill him.' In his autobiography, *Five Times Champion*, Smith later wrote:

The sense of anti-climax and disappointment in the crowd was only too obvious. In the bus going down to the station after racing, passengers were reckoning the sums they would have won in doubles, trebles and accumulators on Gordon's mounts, if Eagle Ray had not been beaten, and were swapping bloodthirsty details of what they would do to the little so-and-so who had ridden Lament if they could lay their hands on him. I practically wrapped myself in the folds of the evening paper and made myself as inconspicuous as possible. But the point they were all overlooking was that Gordon had not even been second, as Cutty Wren beat Eagle Ray by a neck for second place.

If we look around the rest of the world, horse racing history throws up only a handful of statistics comparable to Richards' winning streak. Way back in 1907, at an obscure New Zealand track called Wairoa County, over two days in January, Kiwi jockey Billy Kirk chalked up eleven winners on the trot. In 1958 Sir Gordon's record was reputedly matched by Rhodesian jockey Peter Stroedel. Between 23 August and 3 September 1986 Phil Tuck (formerly the most super-stitious jockey of all until one day he woke up and decided, 'It's all daftness') equalled Johnny Gilbert's 1959 achievement of riding ten consecutive jump winners.

Despite the scarcity of female riders in world racing, a number of women jockeys have already pulled off multiple wins in a day. Britain's Alex Greaves, who has done more than anyone to raise the profile of lady jockeys, won four out of four at Southwell in 1991, at accumula-tive odds of 212/1. What Alex has achieved with persistence and hard work here has been emulated and exceeded in the States by the phe-nomenal Julie Krone riding six winners at Monmouth Park in August 1987. Later in the same year she twice repeated the performance at The Meadowland. Krone describes well the thrill of such days, put-ting them down to 'a combination of a powerful stable, fantastic trainers and the opportunities a winning jockey receives'.

> The jockey has to work her butt off to put herself in a winning situa-tion, but when she rides horses that have a high probability of winning and low odds she is going to win more races. The secret of multiple-win days is to put all those factors together in one day. And when it happens, there is an unbelievable rush and a real sense of power.

If we turn to the statistics for riding the most winners in one day, the British record was set in June 1992 by Pat Eddery, one of the modern era's most successful jockeys, with a total of seven – three at

Newmarket in the afternoon and four more at Newcastle in the evening. In the US the American jockey Chris Antley (who was to die in 2000 in bizarre drug-related circumstances) rode nine winners on 31 October 1987 by doubling up at Aqueduct, New York and The Meadowland, New Jersey out of fourteen rides in all. Hubert Jones rode eight winners in the thirteen-race fixture at Caliente, California in June 1944, while Oscar Barattuci did the same, but with eight consecutive victories, at Independencia, Argentina in 1957. Pat Day's eight from nine at Arlington International, Illinois in 1989 was a pretty special feat, as was Michael Earl Smith winning six from seven twice during January 1992 at the Aqueduct. In Canada Sandy Hawley twice rode seven from nine at Woodbine in the 1970s, and Richard Grubb scored seven from eight there in May 1967. Seven wins from seven rides has been done several times, the earliest by Albert Whittaker in New Zealand in 1910, and most recently by Richard de Pass at Florida Downs in the USA in 1980.

None of these achievements, however, could boast the impact of Frankie's day – with major prizes on offer and live terrestrial television coverage, on the principal day of the racing week with the cream of the day's riding and training talent in action.

'IF THIS ONE WINS,' Frankie told stable lad John Davis before Ascot's next race, 'I'm going to show my bum at the clock tower in Newmarket!'

The second race of the afternoon, the 2.35, was the £100,000 Racal Diadem Stakes, a Group Two, Class A event for three-year-olds and upwards, over 6 furlongs. The Penalty Value was £58,350, second prize £18,990, third £9,446 and fourth £4,560. Originally run in 1946, it was being sponsored by Racal this year for the first time, coinciding with the upgrading of the event to Group Two status.

Davis told Frankie he would follow suit, for the jockey's partner was a horse called Diffident in whom, he later recalled, 'we had no confidence at all'. During the preceding winter the Godolphin four-year-old had won the Presidents Cup in Abu Dhabi, only to run disappointingly on his return, twice finishing down the field. Simon Crisford, Godolphin's manager, nevertheless believed that the horse was in good shape – indeed, had never been better – but worried that he was 'pretty inconsistent'.

However, there was little professional big money support for the colt to bounce back to form. The *Racing Post* reported no substantial bets for him, and Diffident started at odds of 12/1, which made him joint sixth favourite. The punters were going for Lucayan Prince, partnered by Walter Swinburn, who was the 15/8 favourite and carrying some decent bets, including one of £5,000, one of £4,000, two of £3,000 and five of £2,000. Though the race was due off at 2.35, a double-page advertisement in the racecard, promoting Racal 'Communicating through technology', gave the off time as 2.30 – on this particular matter communication had obviously broken down! In the event, both racecard and Racal were wrong, as the race started at 2.36.

Perhaps the signs were already there in the Racal Diadem Stakes that this was to be Dettori's day. Drawn in stall ten, Frankie had the horse handily placed in fifth early on while Pat Eddery made the running on 25/1 outsider Averti. With a furlong to run the race began to take shape. Averti was finding the pace too hot, and unconsidered 66/1 no-hoper Sylva Paradise was taken to the front by Brett Doyle. Leap For Joy came alongside before being urged ahead by Richard Hills as the winning post began to loom. Now Walter Swinburn had finally managed to extricate Lucayan Prince from the traffic problems he had been encountering for most of the race and the pair were eating up the ground. However, while Walter was still moving up through the gears, Frankie had made his move and imparted just enough momentum to his partner to give trainer Saeed bin Suroor his thirty-third winner of the season. The race was run in 1 minute 15.36 seconds. Clive Brittain's Cool Jazz, who had won the race a year earlier, was never in the hunt, finishing distressed in last place. 'It was a slow-run race,' said Frankie, 'but once I found myself some room we flew home and just got there' – though at the same time he admitted that this was the 'most luckiest winner of the year for me'.

Raceform's race reader emphatically agreed: 'Managing to get on top well inside the final furlong, he found the line coming not a stride too soon. There can be absolutely no doubting that, had Lucayan Prince had more luck in running, Diffident would definitely have been second best.' For the *Racing Post* Lucayan Prince was 'the classic example of being all dressed up with nowhere to go'. To be brutally honest, it was Walter Swinburn's decision to drop his mount in on the rails at the rear of the field that appears to have prevented their clear passage at the business end of the race. *Raceform* was prepared to be a little more charitable: 'Unfortunately, [Lucayan Prince] has to be brought with a late run from the back, which means he is always likely to encounter traffic problems. He was the moral victor of this race.' Maybe – but the prize money went to Godolphin. Frankie had ridden Lucayan Prince before; had the Italian not been booked by his stable and done so on this occasion, perhaps that combination would have succeeded again.

An admiring Pat Eddery told me that this was a race which Dettori 'should not have won – it was a case of Frankie at his scintillating best. There are some races,' Eddery went on to explain, 'where it is more the jockey winning than the horse. This was one such race, where Frankie pinched it – he was determined to succeed, and got that extra zip out of his mount.' Despite the closeness of the finish, Frankie always thought he'd held on, as did Peter O'Sullevan who called a photo finish while suggesting that Dettori had narrowly prevailed but subsequently feared he might have used up his ration of good fortune for the afternoon. As he brought the horse back, he raised his right hand almost apologetically as though also acknowledging that he'd enjoyed a little divine assistance.

Tom Kelly, formerly editor of the now-defunct racing paper, the *Sporting Chronicle*, but nowadays poacher-turned-gamekeeper as Director-General of the Betting Office Licensees Association, registered Frankie's second win, but then had to go out for the rest of the afternoon – well away from all news of racing results at Ascot. At this point, anyone with a £1 double riding on the first two winners at

Starting Price odds was congratulating themselves on now having £39 to their credit. Although the bookies hadn't been quite as generous as in the first race, betting to a percentage of 118.8, once again the Tote return underperformed in comparison with the SP, returning £12, or 11/1.

William Hill's David Hood walked down to the rails 'to pass over some bets to our normally ebullient representative, Mike Burton. He was always the loudest operator on the rails and was still in good spirits, although his satchel was taking a bruising from Frankie's double.' Rob Hartnett of Coral had watched the race with mixed feelings: 'Lucayan Prince was the undoubted best horse in the race, who would have won in another half a stride,' he reflected. 'With hindsight, this was our one chance of escape.'

DIFFIDENT: Sire – Nureyev; out of – Shy Princess.

RESULT: 1. Diffident (Dettori) 12/1; 2. Lucayan Prince (W. Swinburn) 15/8f; 3. Leap For Joy (R. Hills); 14/1. 12 ran. Winning distances: short head; short head. Trainer: S. bin Suroor. Tote win return: £12.

CHAPTER FOUR

'THE NUMBER ONE MILER IN EUROPE'

RACEFORM TRIBUTE TO MARK OF ESTEEM

THE FIRST HINT OF potential trouble for bookmakers arrived in the telephone call from the Manchester head office of Fred Done, a bookmaking chain of some 200 betting shops in the north of England, to the boss at home: 'Fred, we've got twenty thousand for Dettori here, and he's ridden the first two already – we don't want a third.'

WHEN ALEC RUSSELL HAD set his record as the first post-war jockey to go through the card, there were, of course, no betting shops at all. Not until almost four years later – on 1 May 1961 – were betting shops legalized in this country. At their peak there were 15,000 shops; today there are fewer than 9,000, as bigger and better-equipped branches have taken over from their predecessors. It was in 1853 that betting shops had originally been banned (in 1850 there were some 400 operating quite legally in London) but then they remained illegal for over a century. The story of the re-emergence of the establishments we now take for granted as the place where most of us place our bets – and which came to play such an instrumental part in Frankie Dettori's historic day – is a fascinating one.

Betting shops first emerged during the first half of the nineteenth century, when popular interest in horse racing was beginning to flourish. On course and credit bookmakers were already well established, but the latter in particular were too concerned with 'gentlemen' clients to worry about lesser fry. However, pioneer betting shop operators, happy to handle small currency penny and 'tanner' bets, set up for business in tobacconists and barber shops – the haunts of men with idle time to kill perusing the sporting papers, and gossiping and gambling. The gambling soon became more significant than the tobacco and haircuts. The interiors of the shops took on a new, prosperous appearance – evidence of where most of the cash was ending up. Carpets and comfortable furniture were brought in to encourage punters to stay. The walls were hung with lists of runners and odds, and the shops became known as list shops or listers.

As they became more profitable, however, so they attracted the attention of criminal types. With the patronage of these less scrupulous characters, so the shops' reputations slumped. By the beginning of the 1850s one estimate put the percentage of betting businesses that were properly run and fully solvent at a mere 4 per cent. At the first sign of a bad result in a big race such dodgy establishments were all too willing to decamp and welsh on their liabilities. Towards the end of 1853, therefore, legislation was introduced to close betting shops down, leading to the rise of an illegal cash betting industry that relied on bookies' runners to collect bets.

A century or so later actual betting shops had begun to appear on the scene again – still against the law, but by now tolerated by the authorities. A *Daily Mirror* article of 1958 revealed how easy it was to place a cash bet. Reporter Jack Stoneley was in Redcar: 'I stopped a policeman and asked, "Please can you direct me to the nearest place where I can put a bet on a horse?" "Certainly, sir,' he smiled, "straight along the road – you'll see a little doorway, just go right in."' Stoneley's piece described how many of the illegal haunts provided telephones, comfortable furniture, TV and radio, refreshments and carpeted floors, as well as relaying commentaries, and displaying odds and runners up on boards. Sometimes the local bobby was even on commission to point would-be punters in the right direction. And, occasionally, just for the sake of appearances, he might pop his head around the door and announce that his superiors had instructed him to raid the establishment. The punishment would be a token fine and warning.

In September 1960 the Home Office announced that betting shops would be allowed to open from 1 May the following year. Not everyone was enthusiastic – the *Daily Mail* reported that 'Mr William Hill, Britain's biggest bookmaker, thinks that only a third of the shops that open will still be in business after a year.' He was spectacularly wrong, of course, and the shops flourished. John Morgan of the *New Statesman* got it right, though, when he wrote that 'With a delicate hypocrisy the government has encouraged gambling by making the shops easily available, but salved its conscience by insisting that they are graceless, utilitarian places without coffee or soft drinks, and even without television to watch the horses.'

Spartan they may have been, but an early pioneer of the shops, John Banks, famously described them as 'a licence to print money'. It was not until 1986 that betting-shop regulations were finally relaxed to permit the installation of TVs and the provision of refreshments for customers. Since then, further improvements to facilities have been allowed. Daily broadcasts of live horse and greyhound racing on banks of screens are supplemented with other live sporting action. Shops are generally spacious and inviting, many air-conditioned, with their windows opened up, and most feature fruit machines. The popularity of the National Lottery is recognized by the introduction of numbers games to bet on, and advertising is permitted. On the other hand, you don't have to visit the shop at all nowadays to place your bet: you can place it readily by phone, via internet betting accounts, or through interactive television. It was overwhelmingly the shops to which the followers of Frankie Dettori like Darren Yates and Pat Epton flocked that day to fill in their betting slips with the names of his seven runners.

FROM THE MOMENT THE betting shops had started to appear on the nation's high streets, bookmakers had quickly learned to fear certain results that could threaten the profits they had perhaps begun to regard as their automatic right. In particular, success for 'public' horses has always been bad financial news for the betting shops and layers, however the bets are placed. Red Rum's third Grand National victory, for example, or Desert Orchid's Cheltenham Gold Cup triumph took millions out of their satchels and tills. Lester Piggott, of course, was the punters' pal for many years. A good day for Lester was a bad day for bookies – and the combination of Lester Piggott and a Classic winner – which happened thirty times, far too many for the layers' liking – was especially damaging. After Dettori had booted home the first two winners at Ascot, there was a horse in the third race that everyone now sensing which way the afternoon was heading would want to back – or, more worryingly for the bookies, had already bought into that morning. And Frankie Dettori was the jockey. Betting shops like Fred Done's were starting to worry.

The 3.20, the Queen Elizabeth II Stakes – a Group One race run over one mile since 1955 – put serious money up for grabs, with an estimated total value of £330,000. Seven of Europe's top milers lined up to do battle for the first prize of £199,020. The second prize was £65,156, third won £32,409 and fourth £15,647. For the winning owner there was also 'a piece of plate' worth £3,000, donated by the Queen herself, along with a 'memento' for the winning owner, trainer and rider. What *Raceform* described as 'undoubtedly the mile Championship race of Europe' had been occupying Frankie's thoughts almost obsessively – 'this was the race I'd been kind of worrying about'. He was determined to win.

Frankie was riding Mark of Esteem, one of the horses caught up in the souring of relations between trainer Henry Cecil and powerful owner Sheikh Mohammed. Cecil had trained the colt as a two-year-old. On his debut at Newmarket he had been beaten by a neck before winning well at Goodwood. His intended autumn target was the Royal Lodge Stakes, but he suffered an injury that coincided with, and perhaps precipitated, the well-publicized split between Cecil and the Sheikh who set up his elite Godolphin project.

Mark of Esteem went off to winter in Dubai, where he regained his fitness and matured. On his return he won the 2000 Guineas at 8/1, a Classic victory that immediately installed him in the ante-post lists of the top bookmakers as a leading candidate for the Derby. Ladbrokes quoted him at just 4/1 – their way of identifying him as a genuine potential winner. But doubts were raised amongst form students as to whether the horse's stamina would allow him to stay the 1½-mile Derby distance, so often the Achilles heel of fancied runners. Mark of Esteem's sire, Darshaan, had won the Prix du Jockey Club in France over 1½ miles, but his dam, Homage, never raced and was a sister to sprinters rather than middle-distance performers.

However, Mark of Esteem became ill with a temperature and had to miss the Derby, thus leaving the distance question hanging unanswered over his handsome head. But a retrospective clue can be gleaned, in as much as the horse's owner and trainer would never ask it to tackle a trip longer than a mile. At Royal Ascot less than a fortnight later, he was beaten comprehensively in the St James's Palace Stakes, an aberration Frankie Dettori excused as Mark of Esteem probably not being quite over his earlier illness.

But the colt bounced back at the end of August with a victory in Goodwood's Tripleprint Celebration Mile, storming home 'in the style of a great horse', according to commentator Mike Cattermole. In that race Frankie had been trapped on the rails by Walter Swinburn – 'in prison' as the Italian put it – but as one horse dropped away, a gap appeared and within a couple of strides Mark of Esteem had imposed himself on the race. 'Once I discovered he had that quick burst of speed,' added Frankie, 'the hardest part was to wait until the furlong pole to release that tremendous turn of foot.'

That form entitled him to serious consideration in the Queen Elizabeth II, despite three-year-old rivals with top-quality credentials. Filly Bosra Sham, ironically enough from the Cecil yard, was a 1000 Guineas winner, while Ashkalani had won the Poule d'Essai des Poulains, and Bijou d'Inde the St James's Palace Stakes. The older opponents were no slouches either. First Island boasted a Sussex Stakes victory, Charnwood Forest had won the Queen Anne Stakes, and Soviet Line was a Lockinge Stakes winner. The prize money accrued by all the contestants was an impressive £2 million.

Despite – or perhaps because of – Frankie's earlier wins, many on-course punters sided with the French horse Ashkalani, who came out of the stalls as 9/4 favourite after attracting one bet of £3,000, four of £2,000 and seven between £1,000 and £1,200. Mark of Esteem and Bosra Sham shared second favourite – the odds of 100/30 suggesting that, as yet, few alarm bells had begun even to tinkle in the headquarters of the big bookies. The largest bets for Frankie's horse were one of £3,000, another of £2,100, three of £1,500, one of £1,000 and seven of £600, as his odds went from 5/2 to 7/2 before levelling off at 100/30. The *Racing Post* noted that this support was 'including office money'.

Mark of Esteem had sweated up in the parade ring, often a bad sign for the race itself. 'He was a little on edge,' said Frankie, 'he could feel the tension of the race.' This may have deterred high-staking racegoers from backing him. Before the race there was then another parade, with the runners led past the stands and back to the winning post before cantering to the start. Mark of Esteem went in last, into stall five, assisted firmly but gently by five stalls handlers. Frankie, says his jockey and colleague Ray Cochrane, 'was a little quiet – he usually makes a lot of noise. I know this because I sat close by him.' At 3.23 the stalls flew open.

In the early stages of the race Mark of Esteem was restrained in fourth or fifth place as Bijou d'Inde dictated the pace under Jason Weaver, together with Bosra Sham who was seeking to become the first filly for some forty years to win this race after triumphing in the Guineas. In the event the race resolved itself into a two-horse contest, as Frankie's mount travelled well throughout, always staying in touch, albeit with four or five lengths to make up as they passed the half mile marker, before being shaken up at the distance and quickening smoothly to pass Pat Eddery on Bosra Sham inside the final furlong. The two joint second favourites pulled four lengths clear of First Island, ridden by Michael Hills, who stayed on for third place.

Well before the finishing post the result was decided, with the vastly experienced – and somewhat crestfallen – Eddery looking round to make sure no one was looming up on the horizon to deprive him of second. 'I honestly thought Bosra Sham was going to win,' Pat later confessed to me. 'I really did think my horse could not lose, but it was a mark of Frankie's riding class that I had to settle for second.' Frankie raised his right hand and flourished his whip even before crossing the line, a delighted expression already spreading across his face. 'An electrifying victory!' Peter O'Sullevan told BBC viewers. Soon the jockey was to echo these sentiments. 'When I asked him,' enthused Dettori, 'the response was electric!'

Frankie pumped his right arm vigorously as he came back. 'He's not exactly showing any signs of disappointment,' observed Peter O'Sullevan dryly. Frankie was mightily impressed with the manner in which the victory was ensured. 'I couldn't believe he was going so well as we passed the furlong marker,' he exclaimed, 'so I decided it was time to go and pulled him out and asked for the effort. The delivery was like a fuel injection – it just knocked me out of my seat! The crowd went ballistic!' Surely this was an occasion worthy of a vintage Dettori flying dismount. But on the way back to the winner's enclosure, a steward approached Frankie to ask him not to perform his trademark celebration. The jockey agreed not to and, as he brought the horse back to a great reception, waggled a finger at the crowd as if to explain that they were to be disappointed. But the ecstatic expressions on the faces of the horse's connections, and the acclaim of the crowd, soon changed his mind. To the great delight of the assembled multitudes (with, I suppose, one or two stewardly exceptions) he duly leaped from Mark of Esteem's back. 'The stewards later told me there was no rule against it but that they were concerned for safety reasons,' he explained. 'If I feel it is not safe with some horses then I wouldn't do it.'

The respected annual publication *Racehorses of 1996* subsequently declared Mark of Esteem to be 'right out of the top drawer', while *Raceform* said the horse 'put up a brilliant display to firmly stamp himself as the number one miler in Europe'. 'A truly outstanding effort,' agreed the *Racing Post*, 'which not only confirms this season's champion miler, but ranks right up there among the very best performances of recent years.'

Looking on as Frankie celebrated victory was the owner of the beaten Bosra Sham, Wafic Said. Betraying none of his own inevitable disappointment, he smiled and congratulated the 'opposition'. 'Wonderful, wonderful,' he declared. 'I'm very, very happy. A marvellous race.' *Sporting Life*'s Monty Court commented, 'I have never seen a beaten owner radiate such joy.' Appropriately enough for a Royal race at the royal racecourse, Princess Alexandra duly added her regal presence to the occasion, handing over the relevant keepsakes to connections. Frankie brandished his trophy triumphantly, and playfully made as if to hurl it towards the spectators.

THIS THIRD SUCCESSIVE DETTORI win produced accumulative odds for the treble of 168/1 and at this point, as the potential implications of one more Dettori win – let alone a possible through-the-card romp – began to sink in, there were furrowed brows in Barking, Harrow and Leeds, the head offices of Coral, Ladbrokes and William Hill. Smaller bookmakers who had taken hundreds of bets on Frankie's mounts involving all sorts of potential combinations were either congratulating themselves on having laid off some of their liabilities to their bigger bookie brethren, or cursing their laziness or lack of foresight at not having done so. But out at the course Coral's Rob Hartnett, while noting that Mark of Esteem had been 'easy to find' for punters, was yet to begin worrying seriously about the outcome of the day for his company. William Hill's David Hood, meanwhile, was seeing more intimations of doom. After his car had been broken into at home that morning, he'd had to arrange for a fitter to come to Ascot to repair the window-glass, and then offer one of the parking attendants a financial inducement to keep an eye on it until he arrived. Now, nipping out to the car park to pick up his car keys, he saw to his dismay that the fitter hadn't turned up.

Bookmakers at Ascot – who are not normally concerned about the number of winners any particular jockey rides (as they rarely take accumulative or permutation bets) – had again bet to a perfectly fair and acceptable 111.9 per cent. Again they had surpassed the Tote, too, where Frankie fans were restricted to a win dividend payout of £3.70.

'I would have settled for the first three winners,' said Frankie when he later came to look back. 'If somebody would have said to me, "You're gonna win the next four," I would have told them they were mad.'

MARK OF ESTEEM: Sire – Darshaan; out of – Homage.

RESULT: 1. Mark of Esteem (Dettori) 100/30; 2. Bosra Sham (P. Eddery) 100/30; 3. First Island (M. Hills) 11/2. 7 ran. Winning distances: 2 lengths; 2 lengths. Trainer: S. bin Suroor. Tote win return: £3.70.

CHAPTER FIVE

'DO YOU THINK ONE JOCKEY CAN AFFECT HORSES IN A WAY THAT PERHAPS OTHER JOCKEYS DON'T?'

BBC's JONATHAN POWELL TO JOHN GOSDEN, TRAINER OF DECORATED HERO

THE BOOKIES NOW KNEW that one more win this afternoon for Frankie meant thousands of punters would be collecting on winning Yankee or Lucky 15 bets.

A Yankee is four selections, backed in a combination of six doubles – i.e. bets on horses A&B, A&C, A&D, B&C, B&D, C&D; four trebles – AB&C, AB&D, AC&D, BC&D; and one four horse accumulator, ABC&D. This bet costs eleven times the unit stake – thus, £11 for £1 units. Add in four singles, one for each of the selections, making fifteen bets in all and you have the Lucky 15 – in which guise it often carries bonuses or consolations for near misses or virtual failure – such as a doubling of the odds should only one of your four selections win. These are possibly the most popular bets for small-money punters, offering an interest in several races for an affordable stake and holding out the prospect of a substantial payout when (or, more usually, if) all four win.

The drawback of the Yankee is that just one losing selection means that seven of the eleven component parts are knocked out; two losers and all that's left is a double on the remaining two. Nevertheless, the bet has proved phenomenally durable, certainly for the forty-year lifetime of betting shops, during which it has been the staple dish on the punter menu.

Those who wanted to cover more than just four of Frankie's rides could have incorporated any six of them in a bet involving a total of fifty-seven bets and therefore known as a Heinz (the much vaunted number of varieties available from that long established brand name), which consists of fifteen doubles, twenty trebles, fifteen fourfolds, six fivefolds and one sixfold.

A Super Heinz goes one better and gives full coverage of every combination possible to incorporate all seven of the races in a total of 120 component parts.

A Super Yankee, or Canadian, consists of five selections in twenty-six different combinations of doubles, trebles and accumulators.

Racecourse bookies do not as a rule handle these bets, sticking to one-off win or each-way wagers and leaving the betting shops on, or off, course to take the vast majority of the multiselection wagers, which are often placed for very small unit stakes. For example, a Goliath bet, involving a full cover of eight selections, 247 elements in all, is beyond the reach of the great majority of gamblers at a £1 unit – but for 1p units it becomes affordable by most at a manageable £2.47 and gives an opportunity to have a stake in every race when eight are being shown on the box.

The derivation of the names of these bets makes for intriguing speculation. In his fascinating *Horse Racing Book of Words*, University of Manchester Reader in English Gerald Hammond advances the theory that 'a yankee may be derived from the idea of a "yankee tournament", one in which everyone plays everyone else'. As for a Canadian, this 'probably derives its name from its being one selection more than a yankee, as Canada is just above the USA'. As for a Goliath – it is 'obviously named after the huge size, massive optimism, and certain failure of the bet,' observes Hammond in deadpan style.

Of course on this day, as on so many others, most betting shop patrons would have placed their Yankees on the first four races of the afternoon – as these were the only ones scheduled for transmission by BBC1. So, should the John Gosden-trained topweight Decorated Hero oblige punters by becoming a fourth consecutive F. Dettori triumph, the black armbands would be brought out of storage in the bookies' cupboards where, apart from the occasional outing in honour of the likes of Red Rum and Desert Orchid, they generally enjoyed a quiet existence.

But there was a little guarded optimism amongst the layers that the 3.55, the £55,000 Tote Festival Handicap (Class B), run over the straight 7 furlong course for three-year-olds and upwards, initiated in 1988 and worth £50,102.50 (Penalty Value) to the winner, £13,265 to the runner-up, £6,632 to the third and £3,324 to the fourth, would be won by a blot on the handicap named High Summer. This horse, trained by Roger Charlton and partnered by Tim Sprake (who has since been continuing his slow recovery from a terrible race fall), was carrying just 8st. 1lb. Following a good performance sixteen days earlier when second behind My Branch in a Listed event at Doncaster last time out, having previously won a Warwick maiden and cruised home in a Salisbury Handicap, she would be asked to carry an additional 20lbs in future handicaps. The three-year-old filly was described as a 'handicap snip [a term first recorded in 1890 according to Hammond] and clear form choice' in the official Ascot racecard, and bookies everywhere were offering up not so silent prayers that she would come to their rescue. The one significant drawback to High Summer's chance was widely glossed over by those fancying her. She had raced with her tongue tied down via a tongue strap and had previously displayed breathing problems.

Frankie, though, wasn't overconfident about his own prospects of winning this race – the one Festival event he had yet to claim. Taking into account a draw that kept him away from the other leading contenders, along with Decorated Hero's 5lb penalty for his recent comeback win after a five month layoff, 'I thought, Jesus, it's going to be an impossible task.'

The race had attracted a turnout of twenty-six runners, and High Summer was a short priced favourite at odds of 5/2. Four-year-old Decorated Hero, carrying not only Dettori but also the accumulated liabilities from his previous three winners into the race, was installed as 7/1 second best, having been available to early backers at 12/1. On-course bookies were having to be careful not to be overgenerous with High Summer's odds, at which shrewd, value seeking gamblers were looking carefully to see whether support for Frankie's bandwagon caused the favourite's price to lengthen. They also had to absorb cash being sent back to the course by anxious betting shop owners, and the effects of these actions were evidenced by the betting percentage of 138.5.

Starting Price Returners Neal Wilkins and Doug Newton noticed early indications of what was to happen in the last race: 'The offices were trying to smash Decorated Hero's price – it touched 11/2 but drifted back to 7/1,' said Wilkins. 'Doug and I were surprised that the horse went off at such comparatively long odds.' Already, therefore, a divergence of requirements and tactics was becoming apparent between the on- and off-course layers.

AS WE HAVE SEEN earlier, the larger bookmaking firms have representatives at a racecourse to ensure that, when necessary, they can place substantial bets with the more influential on-course operators in order to drive down the prevailing odds about runners that could cause them financial damage in the shops. This is an entirely legitimate process, well established over the years, which seeks to prevent the minority of bets influencing the majority and ensures that the Starting Prices returned reflect not only the betting pattern at the course but also the often much greater sums of money placed away from the track around the 8000-plus betting shops of England, Scotland and Wales and also, today, via the internet and in the telephone betting centres.

Many punters criticize this kind of transaction – particularly when it results in the odds about their fancy being shortened up. But it is an essential weapon in an off-course bookmaker's armoury; otherwise they could find themselves exposed to business-threatening liabilities against which they are powerless to defend themselves. There have been numerous examples in the past of strongly fancied horses that have run heavily backed off-course by conspirators. They then endeavoured to force the odds about their target out at the course to odds unrepresentative of its true chances by the simple expedient of betting against that horse on the racecourse where, in a weak market, it can take comparatively little cash to force the price of one or two horses down in the betting, with the result that others start to drift in the opposite direction. In this manner the big money invested away from the track will be settled at those more generous odds.

Of course these coups are equally dependent on the betting shop bosses not twigging that they are being set up for a touch, so the money is spread about and placed in bite-sized pieces. A stranger walking into a betting shop and asking for a three-figure bet on an apparently unfancied horse will raise the odd eyebrow. If that happens a couple of times in different shops and word gets back to headquarters, both eyebrows shoot skyward and moves are made to ensure that the necessary defensive action is taken. Alternatively, those 'in the know' have in the past been a little less subtle in their tactics and just resorted to making sure that the off-course layers have been unable to send money back to the course, whether by utilizing strong-arm methods or by making it impossible to reach the relevant people.

One legendary example of an event of this nature that initially went against the bookmakers occurred in 1953, even before legal betting shops were in existence – which doesn't mean that there weren't a fair number of illegal ones. Santa Amaro and Francasal, both two-year-olds, were imported from France. The former was by far the better of the pair and ran in the name of the latter in a poor race at Bath. There was little money seen for 'Francasal' at the track, but off-course the cash was piling on – an estimated £6,000-plus in total. But bookmakers wishing to get in touch with the course to 'lay off' some of their liabilities discovered that the telephone lines were down – they had been deliberately cut. 'Francasal' bolted home by two lengths at rewarding odds of 10/1. After investigations were instigated, five arrests were made and a trial held, at which the jury failed to agree. A retrial produced four convictions, the longest sentence being three years after evidence from a farrier, a vet, a transporter and trainers eventually yielded proof that the horses had been deliberately switched. All bets on the race were declared void.

A cunningly schemed plot almost landed a £300,000 touch for its perpetrators when a horse called Gay Future won at Cartmel (a small

Lake District course which stages few meetings) on August Bank Holiday Monday 1974. Troon permit trainer Anthony Collins had four horses due to run on the day – Gay Future and Racionzer at Cartmel, Opera Cloak at Southwell, and Ankerwyke at Plumpton. On the morning of the race a group of people set off to place some £30,000 worth of bets on Gay Future – disguising their true intentions by staking mainly £5, £10 or £15 doubles with either Ankerwyke or Opera Cloak. This was an inspired move as bookmakers are normally only suspicious when single horses are backed excessively, and they are far less likely to pay much attention to bets which involve more than one selection and are therefore much less likely to pay off.

However, the sheer volume of bets being placed eventually alerted the bookies, with William Hill going to the unusual extreme of refusing to accept any more bets shortly after midday involving Gay Future or the other two. Collins himself was at Plumpton, ostensibly to look after Ankerwyke. Meanwhile his wife had gone to Cartmel with Gay Future and, importantly, to place on-course bets on Collins's other entry in the same race, Racionzer, clearly to give the impression that this was the more fancied horse of the two, and to keep the price for Gay Future artificially high. Further parts of the plot began to fit into place – the unknown amateur who had been declared as Gay Future's jockey was suddenly replaced by leading Irish amateur Mr T.A. Jones, who had previously ridden Gay Future to victory in Ireland. Before Gay Future entered the parade ring, soap flakes were rubbed into his flanks – making it look like he was sweating up.

The bookies, by now convinced something was amiss but not at all sure just what, had sent representatives to each of the courses at which Collins had entered runners. The men who reached Plumpton were baffled to discover that both Opera Cloak and Ankerwyke had been withdrawn from their races. Cartmel being somewhat remote, the bookies' man sent there failed to arrive on time. Gay Future, making his debut over hurdles, sauntered in by fifteen lengths at odds of 10/1. When horses backed in trebles or doubles fail to run, the win stake money goes on to the remaining selection as a single.

The Betting Office Licensees Association, to which most of the leading off-course bookmakers in the UK belong, advised members to withhold payment of bets on Gay Future, pending the outcome of enquiries into the race. Many smaller companies paid out regardless, but major companies decided to wait – Ladbrokes withheld a reported £10,180, Mecca £14,946, Hills £5,322 and Coral £4,056. It is likely that these figures were an underestimate. BOLA called in Scotland Yard to investigate.

Eventually police took the decision to prosecute. Collins and Irish building contractor William Murphy appeared at Preston Crown Court charged with conspiracy to defraud bookmakers. After a seven day trial, both were found guilty, fined £1,000 and ordered to pay £500 towards prosecution costs, although the judge commented, 'on the facts of the case, the degree of dishonesty is in my assessment, although a conspiracy to defraud, very much at the bottom end of the scale'. Following the outcome, the *Sporting Life* (the Sport of Kings' bible at the time) ruled that all bets on the race won by Gay Future were void. BOLA advised members to return stakes and, after a six month period, to donate any unclaimed to a racing charity.

The main point brought out by the prosecution during the case was that the conspirators had never intended for Opera Cloak or Ankerwyke to take part in the races for which they had been entered – this was just a subterfuge to enable them to back Gay Future without drawing attention to the fact. Whatever the whys and wherefores of this case, Gay Future himself enjoyed no happy ending – he suffered a fatal fall during a hurdle race at Wetherby three weeks before the Preston trial.

A year after the Gay Future affair, the Yellow Sam coup also created a stir as another implacable scourge of the layers set about exploiting the betting system's loophole. Five-year-old gelding Yellow Sam was trained for Mrs Maureen Curley at The Curragh by Liam Brennan and had little form of note to his credit when he went to post for a race at Bellewstown on 25 June 1975. Ridden by Michael Furlong, and available at 20/1 on course, bookmakers who suddenly discovered they had taken numbers of bets of up to £50 a time for the horse were unable to get in contact with on-course layers as the one public telephone was – purely coincidentally (!) – permanently occupied by a large gentleman who had apparently suddenly been informed that a close relative was seriously ill and therefore he had to keep in permanent contact with the relevant hospital from the only available phone. As a result, no money could get back to the track. There were, though, an awful lot of fingers dialling out that number in desperation – a team of a dozen trusted putters-on had targeted up to 150 betting shops. Yellow Sam's two-and-a-half length victory resulted in a 20/1 starting price.

Maureen Curley's husband, Barney Curley, whose kindness to Dettori we have already recorded, but who became subsequently the bane of bookmakers everywhere as a trainer-punter, was estimated – in Curley's own autobiography, *Giving A Little Back* – to have netted £300,000 as a result of the horse's victory. The fate of the large gentleman's sick relative is not recorded. Had the chap's ailing family member not been thus stricken at such a vital time, it is probable that the off-course liabilities would have made it into the course market, thus bringing about a rapid reduction in the odds being offered about Yellow Sam from the 20/1 forever in the form book to a more accurate 2/1 or thereabouts. Curley, who once sought to enter the spartan Jesuit order, later commented, 'It was quite simply one man's brains against the bookmakers. There was nothing illegal about it, and I never considered there was anything immoral about it.' Today, mobile phones and improved technology mean that communication is very much easier than even a few years ago, so it is ever more difficult for plotting punters to put one over on the old enemy. Not that they will ever stop trying.

DECORATED HERO, READ RACEGOERS in their £1 racecard, 'faces a stiff task under top weight' of 9st. 13lbs. But he had won at Doncaster a fortnight earlier, charging home like the proverbial locomotive powered vehicle, and, in this very race a year earlier, he and Frankie had finished second in a field of twenty-seven runners at odds of 10/1, behind 20/1 chance, the Geoff Lewis-trained Night Dance, an absentee today. Therefore many backers would consider Frankie's mount a viable each-way option, even though 7/1 was three points under the odds predicted in that racecard. However, the horse had been available early on at 12/1, and halved in price before retracting back one point. Bets 'including office money' were logged of £1,400 to win £10,000 four times, and of £700 to win £5,000 five times.

Frankie, wearing white silks with red cross belts, white sleeves with red diamonds and a red and white hooped cap, was drawn in stall number 22. As the jockeys concentrated, ready to jump their horses off to a good start, there was a brief delay as My Gallery reared up in the stalls. Once they were released, four minutes late at 3.59, My Best Valentine, the favourite High Summer and Primo Lara bounced out in front, with Sabot also well there. Dettori, running out wide and two-thirds of the way down the field, was content to let the race pan out in front of him. Making steady headway from 2 furlongs out, he brought Decorated Hero into contention, executing the decisive move brilliantly – gliding purposefully yet carefully so as not to obstruct any other runner, across towards the stands side of the course. He hit the front with a furlong to go and ran on well to land a convincing three and a half length victory from 20/1 shot Kayvee, who had finished third in the race in both 1993 and 1994. As Frankie sweeps through to win, the video of the race clearly picks out a young boy in a white shirt hurtling down towards the rails to catch a glimpse of the finish, little realizing that he is becoming a small part of racing history in the making.

'He's done it again!' declared Peter O'Sullevan in what came as close to unrestrained excitement as he ever allowed to creep into a commentary. 'It's a four-timer!' Julian Wilson was full of admiration for the race-riding technique: 'Frankie had to thread his way through and had plenty to do.' For the *Racing Post* it was 'a cracking performance under a big weight'.

Now even the bigger boys amongst the bookies were beginning to feel a twinge of apprehension. 'Everyone woke up to the fact that this was a bad day for the book,' recalled Coral's Rob Hartnett with a certain amount of understatement. 'Decorated Hero put my phone on red alert.' In the press room the 'hacks' had woken up to the possibility of a big story. 'The first time what was to become the most repeated question of the season was asked,' says David Hood of William Hill, 'came when Chris McGrath of *The Times*, with a suspiciously wry smile, crowed, "How much is this costing you?"'

But the big shock of the race was the dismal display of the hotly fancied High Summer, who finished ahead of only six runners, occupying an inauspicious twentieth position, despite having flattered to deceive by being up with the pace for half a mile. Jockey Tim Sprake later reported that she had been fine while they had been bowling along in the early stages, but as soon as the pressure was applied, 'she started to gurgle and stopped quickly'. This was endorsed by trainer Roger Charlton, and the stewards ordered a routine test on the horse. She had clearly suffered a recurrence of her breathing problems and, in fact, did not reappear on a racecourse for the remainder of the season.

Decorated Hero had been bred by two well-known racing figures, who now qualified for the race's Breeder's Prize of £1,518. Reg Griffin was one of the key personalities at the Timeform rating operation; Jim McGrath (not to be confused with 'Aussie' Jim, J.A. McGrath, who writes on racing for the *Daily Telegraph* and on this day was working as the racecourse commentator) is familiar to TV viewers for his contributions to Channel 4's racing coverage. Renowned as a shrewd punter, McGrath had invested 'a few quid' of his own on Decorated Hero, although he had felt the horse was not well drawn and had rather blotted its copybook by winning last time out, which had meant it was running here with top weight. It had, though, been laid out for the race. McGrath was well satisfied: 'Frankie rode a beautiful race and dictated the tactics,' he said. The victory made him look forward even more to the sale in a few days' time of a Lahib yearling he and Griffin had also bred, which just happened to be a half brother to Decorated Hero. The horse was subsequently bought by Sheikh Hamdam for

65,000 guineas. Named Mubrik, it went on, coincidentally, to finish fourth in this same Tote Handicap two years later.

Frankie came back to the enclosure waving and holding up four fingers. '*Four!*' he mouthed. He clapped his hands theatrically over his ears as though to shield them from the decibels of the welcoming crowd. This time he resisted the clear temptation to leap off the horse, instead sliding off to shake hands with John Gosden and pat the horse affectionately on the head. The trilby-clad trainer in turn slapped him on the back. Now Gosden was interviewed by the BBC's Jonathan Powell. 'Bookmakers are already crying with pain with the efforts of Frankie Dettori,' was how Powell introduced their conversation, before asking the handler if he agreed that certain jockeys 'can affect horses in a way that perhaps other jockeys don't?'

Gosden, for his part, was naturally complimentary about Dettori's contribution to the victory, revealing that the jockey had carried out perfectly their pre-arranged plan. 'He rode a very cool race. They went very fast on the stand side. He sat off them, rode his own race, which we decided we were going to do, came through, and won. If you ask me,' added Gosden, 'if Frankie Dettori is the best jockey – emphatically, yes.' Gosden also let it slip that earlier in the week Frankie had been a little under the weather with a cold, and had taken himself off to a health club. 'Rather than just lay about the house, he went and got himself organized. Riding a horse you've got to be phenomenally fit and strong – and jockeys are riding below their natural body weight, which is probably what so many people don't realize.'

The presentations after the race were made by the Chairman of the Tote, Lord Wyatt of Weeford, better known as Woodrow Wyatt. Wyatt, however, managed the remarkable feat of not finding anything remotely noteworthy about the day – making no reference to it whatsoever in Volume 3 of his *Journals* (although he did record having been at Ascot on the Sunday). The accumulative odds for Frankie's first four were now up to 1,351/1. The Tote Return for Decorated Hero was £9.30.

Extraordinarily, after this fourth race some spectators decided to head off home – a decision many of them would regret long afterwards. To me, early defection like this, from any sporting event, is incomprehensible. Indeed, the last ten minutes of a football match are statistically the most likely to produce a goal – but still you regularly see people slipping away even when the scores are level. I mention this in order to report that, amazingly, several prominent racing journalists, including one from one of our most respected broadsheets, had also zoomed off for the exit – only for one or two to tiptoe quietly back when the enormity of the breaking story they were missing sank in. Any suggestions from four separate sources that among them was Richard Edmondson of the *Independent*, a man who has frequently written critically about bookmakers, were purely speculative, until he plucked up the courage to ring me to confess that he was an early departee.

MEANWHILE, FRED DONE, PROPRIETOR of the sizeable bookmaking chain that bore his name, was digesting the implications of Dettori's fourth win. 'I knew we were in trouble,' he says simply, 'when, for the first time in twenty years, I was called back to Head Office.'

DECORATED HERO: Sire – Warning; out of – Bequeath.

RESULT: 1. Decorated Hero (Dettori) 7/1; 2. Kayvee (A. Clark) 20/1; 3. Russian Music 16/1 (M.J. Kinane); 4. Ramooz (W. Swinburn) 12/1. Winning distances: 3½ lengths; ½ length; ½ length. Trainer: J. Gosden.

CHAPTER SIX

'I THINK I'LL KEEP THE LINES UP. YOU NEVER KNOW – FRANKIE
MIGHT HAVE RIDDEN A FEW WINNERS'

GRANDSTAND's DAVID GORDON

THE BBC WERE SCREENING the day's Festival of Racing at
Ascot. Even before racing began, the programme presenter
Julian Wilson seems – for some reason that still eludes him – to
have had a subconscious inkling that something was going to
happen that afternoon. 'We were due to cover live the first four
races, but I asked David Gordon [the editor of *Grandstand*] about the
technicalities of recording the last three races. Normally, after the
end of our transmission the BT sound lines are relinquished to save
money. "Oh, I think I'll keep the lines up," said David. "You never
know – Frankie might have ridden a few winners!" I laughed – "I
can't see him riding more than two."' Thanks to this remarkable piece
of foresight, the Beeb was now able to stay on air after the fourth race
to watch the drama unfold.

Nevertheless, now that that fourth race was over, its celebrated
race commentator Peter O'Sullevan was thinking he had finished
work for the afternoon. No one had told him that any more than the
scheduled four races would be broadcast. He had talked Decorated
Hero home and now believed his stint was finished and his duty done.
According to one BBC insider, at this point Peter was already on his
way to the gates, to get ahead of the crowds. 'I'm always the first out
of a course,' he subsequently told Sir Clement Freud in a *Racing Post*
interview. But the great man personally scotches such a heinous suggestion: 'I left my commentary position,' he told me, 'and decided,
quite exceptionally, to go to the BBC Hospitality box to enjoy a drink
with a friend of mine. Meanwhile, producer Martin Hopkins had

decided to extend the BBC's coverage and sent people off to scour the racecourse to let me know. They searched all over, assuming I must have left, and eventually decided they would have to call in the more than capable John Hanmer. I went off to watch the next race – and was surprised to discover what had happened.'

Hanmer was not too surprised to be drafted in. 'I frequently assisted Peter, and I know he was always reluctant to cover races at short notice if he hadn't been able to do his homework. I can only remember him breaking that rule once – for a race in which Princess Anne was competing. I was happy to take over, as I was familiar with the majority of the horses competing in the last three races.' What John was not aware of – and was surprised to discover when I spoke to him in February 2001 – was that these fifth and sixth races were going to be screened live.

UP IN MORECAMBE, DARREN Yates had turned out that Saturday afternoon as centre-half for his local football team. They'd crashed to a 4–0 defeat. Unaware of how his bet was progressing, he had popped into a local pub afterwards to drown his sorrows. 'When I got to the pub,' he remembers, 'they said Dettori had four out of four. I reckoned I'd already won £700.'

FATE HAD INDEED ALREADY decided to make a dramatic intervention in what had started out as a routine day's sport. So what could be a better omen for Frankie's chances in the next race than his horse's name? For Fatefully, Frankie's fifth mount, the racecard confidently predicted odds of 5/1. But considering the enormous, and ever-increasing potential payouts now faced by the layers, indeed, even had all Dettori's previous four rides failed to win, it is difficult to imagine that such a generous price was ever likely. On all available form the horse was entitled to be considered a major player in the race, and with hindsight those odds look more like wishful thinking by a prospective backer than a genuine pointer to its real prospects.

The racecard also pointed out that the Godolphin filly, a bay three-year-old trained by Saeed bin Suroor, was 'useful and improving' so, despite being raised in weight by 7lbs for a recent win, she was always going to be the likely favourite in this company. While most morning papers more accurately made her clear favourite, later Frankie said he was not too sure Fatefully should have been market leader; he had 'a very open mind' about the outcome. He must have cast his mind back, though, to 12 June 1996 when a ten-ride double stint at Yarmouth and Kempton had yielded a total return of six winners, three at each meeting – and one of them was Fatefully.

The 4.30 was the Class A Rosemary Rated Stakes, a one mile handicap for fillies of three years old and upwards, with £19,129.20 prize money to the winner. Eighteen runners lined up to contest the race, run over the straight mile course used for the Royal meeting's famous Royal Hunt Cup. Frankie was in the familiar Godolphin Royal Blue silks. In her previous three races Fatefully had won twice: a handicap at Sandown over an extended mile eleven days earlier (when she had been ridden by John Reid), and a 7 furlong Yarmouth maiden.

Drawn low, in stall six, the filly was backed to 7/4 favourite at the off. Her odds had touched as long as 5/2 and as short as 13/8 (the final betting percentage was 133.4, showing clearly that the bookies were no longer inclined to be overgenerous). All of them had columns and columns of bets for Fatefully, and of all sizes. There were four bets between £14,000 and £8,000, three between £10,000 and £5,000, fourteen bets of £4,000, three of £3,000, seven of £2,000, and five of £1,000! Not surprisingly, these sums included a considerable amount of money sent to the course by the off-course betting shop head offices. Here, as controlled panic was setting in, up to £250,000 (in the informed guesstimate of *Sporting Life*'s Doug Nelson) was diverted away from the vaults and towards the course. 'Get what you can on to kill the price,' was the gist of the mobile messages curtly delivered to the bookies' men at the track.

The runners got away to a level break two minutes later than scheduled. Frankie dropped Fatefully into the leading group in about sixth place, while the early leader, Ninia, battled it out up front with Min Alhawa, Supamova and Questonia. Ray Cochrane was on Abeyr, a 25/1 outsider but the horse he fancied best out of his three rides that day. He sat in and settled mid-field, watching the pack in front of them as they made their way up the long Ascot hill. 'They were going a good pace,' says Cochrane, 'great, Frankie was up the sharp end. They picked it up about two and a half out and I moved through the field.' Fatefully had squeezed through a narrow gap to take the lead below the distance (240 yards from the finish); Frankie was in front. Now Cochrane, in Sheikh Ahmed Al Maktoum's yellow silks with black epaulets, galvanized Abeyr to run on strongly. Behind this pair, Pat Eddery on Questonia had to tug at his mount's head as Frankie and Fatefully drifted slightly towards the rail. 'A furlong to go,' recalls Ray Cochrane, 'I was about one length down and closing on him. I thought I would get him, but he had kept a bit up his sleeve.' It was a driving finish: Abeyr forced Frankie to pull out all the stops. All the way to the line the crowd had gathered along the rails to urge him on, many of them jumping up and down in their excitement and enthusiasm. Fatefully hung on for victory by a mere neck – the third shortest of all margins of victory. In just 1 minute 41.76 seconds Frankie had now made what TV commentator John Hanmer was greeting as a 'fantastic five-timer'. 'As we pulled up, the horses were very close,' Ray Cochrane recalls, 'I said, "Is anyone else getting a chance today?" He roared back, "I'm on fire, mate!"'

'I was just waiting for something to come and beat me,' said Dettori afterwards. 'Ray came to my girth but my filly just pulled out a little bit more.' 'She's an improving filly, but this is as good as she is' was the post-race verdict on Fatefully from Godolphin's Simon Crisford. Abeyr had been carrying 5lbs more than Fatefully; perhaps that had just tipped the balance. The runner-up was bred by Willie Carson, who was following the action on TV from his hospital bed having only just come out of intensive care, after being badly injured a week earlier in the paddock at Newbury when he was kicked by a filly, his injuries including a lacerated liver. But had he been at Ascot, Frankie was in no doubt what the diminutive former champion's reaction would have been: 'He'd have given me a big bollocking!' One and three-quarter lengths behind the first two horses came the 33/1 chance Prancing, ridden by Olivier Peslier.

Even as Fatefully was coming past the winning post, BBC Radio's racing commentator Peter Bromley had been writing a piece for broadcast about the afternoon. *Sport on Five* was broadcasting live second-half commentary of the 'Old Firm' Scottish derby game between Rangers and Celtic, and Bromley's racing round up was due to go out at the end of the match. 'You might have to wait to file that piece,' said a member of his production staff. 'If Frankie wins the next, you'll have to change that five-timer to six.'

IT WAS THE RESULT Rob Hartnett had feared – £1 accumulators were now worth £3,718 – though he hadn't actually watched it happen. Now the experienced, normally unflappable man from Coral was 'in a huddle with other members of the Coral team, wondering what we could do to minimize the damage'. This time the Tote return of £3 exceeded the Starting Price odds. Frankie and his horse made the by now familiar walk into the winner's enclosure, the jockey raising his right hand with fingers spread, signifying, 'Five out of five!' He climbed down from Fatefully's back to an audible sigh of disappointment that there was no theatrical dismount. 'He'll have to do it if he gets six,' said a spectator whose voice was picked up by the TV microphones. Dettori strode off to weigh in and ran into Ian Balding, the trainer of his mount in the next race. 'I hope you haven't used up all your luck,' was Balding's greeting.

Suddenly there was a moment of drama at Ascot. An announcement came over the public address, and up on the course's number boards went a red flag with a white 'E': a stewards' enquiry had been called to look into the possibility that Fatefully may have veered to her left, causing interference to other horses. A quorum of three stewards, chaired by M.C.C. (Mark) Armitage, went into session to review the race on video. There was a nervous wait as they scrutinized possible interference one and a half furlongs out.

Eventually, they found that Frankie's mount had indeed interfered with Questonia (ridden by Pat Eddery), but concluded that it had been accidental, and therefore the race placings should remain unaltered. Their decision was signalled on the number boards by a white flag – as though the stewards, soon to be followed by the bookies, were surrendering before Frankie's irresistible advance.

In the offices of the *Sporting Life*, racing's paper of record for nearly 150 years, a heated discussion was in progress. Acting editor Ben Newton had earmarked a report of Mark of Esteem's victory as the front page lead. On the other hand, the long-serving Jeremy Chapman, who was also something of an expert on betting matters, was arguing that the feat of riding five, possibly more, consecutive winners already outranked any one race, no matter how important. Eventually, says Chapman, 'I convinced Ben the story had to be the lead, whether or not Frankie got five, six or seven, because it was such a mega race meeting and all the Dettori accumulators and cross-doubles would give us a great betting story, even if he failed to get all seven.' Thus the *Sporting Life* (as you'll see from the back cover of this book) managed to avoid devoting its lead story to just one (albeit significant) race, and hold the front page for the really big story.

Like the *Life*'s editor Tom Clarke, Radio 5 Live's racing presenter Cornelius Lysaght was also enjoying a rare Saturday off, in this case to attend the wedding of 5 Live's motor racing correspondent Jonathan Legard. Around 4.30 p.m. Legard was just getting to his feet at the reception to begin his speech. 'Jonathan announced the sports report headlines relevant to people in the room,' remembers Lysaght, 'and he declared that Dettori had already won five races at Ascot. "Ho, ho, ho!" We roared with derision – a likely story!'

One result that didn't make it into Legard's wedding speech, or indeed Radio 5 Live's sports headlines, was that the amateur rugby side Harwell had just received 'a damned good thrashing'. Nevertheless, Michael Caulfield had enjoyed himself turning out for his local side, and now, having changed and showered, he nipped across to the pub for a pint. There he was very surprised to discover that racing was still on the television – and even more surprised when he discovered that one of the members of the organization of which he is executive manager was making headlines. For Michael is the top man in the Jockeys' Association, and as such, the man who fights the riders' battles on the important issues in their working lives. 'I soon became aware that this was a completely freakish day.'

Up at Fred Done's they'd now put a message out to their shops: 'Only let us know about liabilities of £5,000 or more', as the head office tried to estimate the bookmaker's exposure. Done was fearing the worst – but no one knew what the worst might be.

In her London hotel Mary Bolton was feeling the tension as her fifth selection obliged. She couldn't bear to watch the television any longer, so she went out for a walk.

FATEFULLY: Sire – Private Account; out of – Fateful.
RESULT: 1. Fatefully (Dettori) 7/4F; 2. Abeyr (R. Cochrane) 25/1; 3. Prancing (O. Peslier) 33/1; 4. Questonia (P. Eddery) 8/1. 18 ran. Winning distances: Neck; 1¾ lengths; 1¼ lengths. Trainer: S. bin Suroor.

CHAPTER SEVEN

'WHAT A SMUG BASTARD!'

A CHILI RESPONSE TO FRANKIE

BACK IN THE 1930S the actress Chili Bouchier became known to filmgoers as the Brunette Bombshell. In September 1996 Ms Bouchier was now a well-preserved eighty-seven years of age and living in Marylebone, London. She had also been flattered to discover that a two-year-old filly – a 12,000-guinea yearling trained by Doug Marks (who had in the past trained for the likes of Jimmy Tarbuck and Frankie Vaughan) – had been named after her, and was making its debut at Ascot on Saturday 28 September.

Chili – the actress, that is – decided, therefore, to visit her local betting shop to watch her namesake in action and, although it was ranked as a 66/1 outsider, risk £5 on its chances. She may have been the only person in the whole country who watched the sixth race at Ascot that afternoon *not* interested in the fortunes of Frankie Dettori.

One of Frankie's most appealing qualities is his ability to come up with the quotable off-the-cuff quip despite English evidently not being his native language. After he had teamed up with one of the most popular sprinters in training, the flying bay mare Lochsong – twice winner of the unofficial sprint championship of Europe, Longchamp's Prix de l'Abbaye – to spread-eagle the field in the 1993 Nunthorpe Stakes at York, he memorably described her as being 'like Linford Christie without the lunchbox'. The association with Lochsong and her notoriously lucky owner Jeff Smith, the Chairman and Chief Executive of the AIM Group plc, who at that time had some thirty horses in training with twenty-two brood mares kept at the Littleton Stud, did no harm at all to Frankie's burgeoning reputation, and she remains one of his favourite partners.

For Ascot's sixth race of the afternoon, the 5.00, Frankie was teamed up with Lochsong's half-sister, the chestnut Lochangel, also owned by Jeff Smith, and trained at Kingsclere by Ian Balding.

Ian's daughter, Clare, the television presenter for the BBC's racing coverage, was at the course working for the BBC Radio 5 Live team with commentator Peter Bromley because the usual presenter, Cornelius Lysaght, had gone to Jonathan Legard's wedding. It was one of the first major racing events she had presented for 5 Live on her own, though she still modestly describes herself as 'such a small player on the day'. She certainly hadn't expected still to be covering the racing this late in the proceedings, but of course this was anything but a normal afternoon.

Clare and Frankie went back a long way. 'He used to come round to the house with me and my brother Andrew,' she remembers. 'He'd eat everything in the fridge and Dad would make us sit through old videos of Mill Reef [the great 1971 Derby winner he had trained].' The first time Frankie was due to stay the night at the Baldings, she adds, her Uncle Willie – trainer Lord Huntingdon – 'told him to lock his bedroom door, because I was a nymphomaniac'. Clare had already interviewed her old friend three times that Saturday afternoon: before he won on Mark of Esteem, again after Decorated Hero's victory, and yet again following his win on Fatefully. Now, with history being made and Frankie due to ride a horse her father had trained in the next race, she was petrified that 'Dad would let the whole thing down'.

Having checked in with the BBC studio to let them know where she was, she went down to the parade ring. 'Dad was getting tense and was pessimistic. I saw Michael Stoute, trainer of Frankie's seventh ride, and told him, "If we win, the pressure's on you, mate." He didn't think Fujiyama Crest was going to win.'

Meanwhile, 5 Live was now having to consider taking the almost unprecedented step of delaying the classified football results on its flagship *Sports Report* show, so as to be able to carry on live commentary of the sixth race. The editor that day, Joanne Watson, was well aware of the drama unfolding at Ascot. However, ultimately – some might say, amazingly – she decided that 'nothing makes way for James Alexander Gordon reading the football results, so I had the main headlines reporting Frankie's performance but decided against taking the race live'. Such is the inaccuracy of our memories, despite the impact of the day, that several people maintained to me that the football results had actually been delayed.

Liam McGuigan, the Operations Director for William Hill, was shopping in Bishops Stortford when he was alerted that Frankie was now on five. Aware of the financial implications, he began to make plans immediately. 'We were part of Brent Walker at the time,' explains John Brown, the Managing Director, 'and they were in a difficult financial situation – under the management of a group of banks who were controlling the company. It was essential there was no suggestion that we wouldn't be able to pay.' Arrangements were put in place to ensure rapid payment of all bets.

The sixth race was the Class B 6f Blue Seal Conditions Stakes, with £20,000 added to stakes, and worth £12,335.50 to the winner. Only four opponents confronted Lochangel, but one of them, Corsini (trained by Henry Cecil), who had won her only previous race, a maiden at Lingfield, had been tipped to start as odds-on favourite. Indeed, Corsini, due to be ridden by Pat Eddery, opened up at 4/5 but then retreated out to 11/8 at one stage. Under normal circumstances Lochangel could have been expected to trade at around 2/1 or maybe 3/1, but eventually both Dettori's and Eddery's mounts ended up as the 5/4 joint favourites.

John Brown, at Ascot entertaining clients, had gone down to the betting ring to find Mike Burton, his firm's on-course representative, and warn him to keep Lochangel's offered odds as short as possible – a case of teaching grannies to suck eggs if ever there was one. On the way he had bumped into Alastair Down, the racing writer who is also a member of Channel 4's racing team. 'Alastair asked me what I thought of the situation,' says Brown. 'I told him, "It's definitely a brown trouser job."'

Betting on this penultimate race, however, was going in two directions. The professional punters and their high-rolling counterparts were taking advantage of Corsini's apparently overgenerous odds, with bets on her of £1,000, £2,000, £3,000, £4,000 and £6,000 placed. On the other hand, the 'ordinary' racegoers were playing up the profits they had made on Frankie so far. As the off-course bookies detected ever-increasing numbers of accumulative and multiple wagers, therefore, they were anxious to depress Lochangel's price.

Bets logged for Lochangel by the *Racing Post* included a hefty £16,000 to win £20,000 (5/4), a £12,000 stake, another of £10,000, three of £8,000, eleven of £4,000 each and dozens of smaller yet still substantial wagers. Of the other runners Dust Dance, the mount of Richard Quinn, had been anticipated as the second favourite to Corsini, but now there was lukewarm support for it among the punters and it drifted alarmingly from 6/1 out to 12/1, levelling off at 11/1. Plaisir d'Amour, trained by Neville Callaghan, who had cost IR 130,000 guineas, was widely expected to improve for the experience of this first appearance (for the uninitiated, this is often a euphemism for 'unlikely to be given the toughest of rides'), and at the available 15/2 odds duly attracted little in the way of substantial bets. The other debutante, the Brunette Bombshell's namesake, Chili Bouchier, looked on breeding to be in over her head, an assessment reflected in her 66/1 price. The total betting percentage at the off was 110.5 per cent – which even the harshest critic of bookmakers, Paul Haigh of the *Racing Post*, would be hard-pressed to criticize.

On her first time out, at Kempton Park in a fillies' maiden race over 6 furlongs in which she was very slowly away, Lochangel had finished second, going down by four lengths to Blane Water. Frankie, showing the professionalism you would expect, had spoken to her rider that day, Martin Dwyer, and been told that Lochangel had run really 'green' or inexperienced. She had missed the break and lost many lengths in the early stages but, once she got the hang

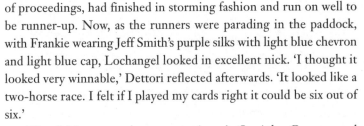

of proceedings, had finished in storming fashion and run on well to be runner-up. Now, as the runners were parading in the paddock, with Frankie wearing Jeff Smith's purple silks with light blue chevron and light blue cap, Lochangel looked in excellent nick. 'I thought it looked very winnable,' Dettori reflected afterwards. 'It looked like a two-horse race. I felt if I played my cards right it could be six out of six.'

The 5.00 was to be run on Ascot's Straight Course, and Lochangel, sporting a white sheepskin noseband, was drawn in stall number five. After the race, the word was that Ian Balding had wanted Frankie to drop the horse in and hold her up for a late run. But as the horses went off bang on time, Frankie opted to make the running. 'That's the difference between a good jockey and a great one,' thought an impressed Clare Balding – no slouch on a horse herself. 'He could assess a situation in a split second,' she explains, 'and had the confidence to change the plan if necessary.'

'Pat's getting quite serious on Corsini,' John Hanmer was saying in his television commentary. But Lochangel was showing that she had learned some track craft from her debut by running on well along the rails to hold off a determined Eddery. The two principals drew five lengths clear of Dust Dancer, who was a further two and a half lengths ahead of Plaisir d'Amour. Without ever quite threatening to get her head in front, Corsini made Lochangel battle all the way to the line. As the two horses came well inside the final furlong on their dash for the post, several balloons hovering over the rails hinted at the celebrations to come.

Up went Frankie's right hand as he realized he'd equalled the record set by Willie Carson, Gordon Richards and Alec Russell. Clutching his whip and punching the air in triumph, he crossed the finishing line. Chili Bouchier, always behind, struggled across the line some six lengths behind the other horses.

Because it was just after 5 p.m., on Radio 5 Live Ian Payne was reading out the *Sports Report* headlines. 'Frankie's had five out of five,' he began. 'No, make that six out of six.' At this point Joanne Watson decided she did have to re-arrange the programme to accommodate live commentary of the final race.

Cheers rang out as Frankie returned to the winner's enclosure yet again, beaming, laughing and gesturing in disbelief. He clapped his hands high above his head and jumped off the horse. Even the three elderly, bowler-hatted officials standing behind him, usually so impassive, could not resist breaking into spontaneous applause. Fellow jockeys came out to greet and congratulate Frankie; the crowd was buzzing with excitement and anticipation. 'A dream,' was Frankie's simple verdict.

In a betting shop in Marylebone, however, and watching Frankie celebrating on the television screen, Chili Bouchier had not taken defeat well. Unaware of what had gone before, she turned to her companion and snapped, 'Look at him leaping about and grinning all over his face. What a smug bastard!'

Behind the scenes someone had been on the ball, and now, at a hastily organized presentation, Colonel Sir Piers Bengough, KCVO, OBE, DL, the Queen's representative at Ascot, was able to hand over a magnum of champagne to a grateful Frankie and hoist the jockey's arm aloft like a newly crowned boxing champion. (Ascot's Racecourse Director, Douglas Erskine-Crum, CBE, later explained to me that the course had wanted to mark the deed at this point because with his sensational sextet Frankie had already set an Ascot record. 'It would have been something of an anti-climax had we waited until after the last and he then hadn't won it!') Frankie grabbed a microphone and spoke excitedly to the crowd before giving a brief interview to BBC *Grandstand* presenter Sue Barker.

Those punters capable of keeping track of a fast escalating accumulator bet now knew that a £1 Frankie wager was worth £8,365.50 at SP odds. Rob Hartnett of Coral was beginning to despair: 'Our best hope of a saviour, Corsini, never got to her rival.' Frankie's friend, bookies' *bête noire* and racing maverick, Barney Curley had seen quite enough for one day and decided to leave. 'I just felt he couldn't do it on Fujiyama Crest,' he remembers. 'I left the racecourse and went

down to a betting shop in nearby Windsor to watch the last, still not
thinking he would win.' They were sentiments with which the bookmakers on the course would have heartily agreed, and Barney explains
why. 'They're not noted for being people with feelings – they were
playing the percentages.'

At Fred Done's they had already taken an important trading decision. 'I decided not to hedge a penny – I can stand a decent bet –
although I still didn't know our liability.' And while Darren Yates was
calculating that his bet was now 'heading for the £27,000 mark', on a
beach in Majorca a North London bookmaker was being paged by 'a
rather distressed hotel bell boy', concerned to inform him that, 'There
is a man from London screaming for you on the phone.' The object of
all this panic, John Nelson, was not only the owner of two betting
shops, but also deputy chairman of the British Betting Office
Association, who had decided to reward himself for a recent stint of
hard work with a fortnight in the sun. The voice on the telephone
belonged to Doug, his General Manager. 'John! John!' came the
plaintive voice in his ear – 'I've done [lost] the business . . .!'

'Calm down and explain,' ordered a bewildered Nelson. So Doug
told him about Frankie's six winners, then gave him the devastating
news that they had some £55,000 running on to Fujiyama Crest and
were unable to lay off their liabilities anywhere. 'Call the Tote,'
instructed Nelson. 'Get as much as possible on at Tote odds.'

Nelson's instruction demonstrated the desperate situation he
knew they were in. A hefty wager at Tote odds would to a certain
extent be self-defeating, because it would inevitably cut his potential
pay-out. But he just wanted to limit his exposure by any means available. However, even these desperate means, it was to transpire, were
no longer available to him.

Incredibly, given that, like a lottery, the Tote can never pay out
more than it takes in, Nelson says it refused his bet. 'They kept
making excuses, but couldn't come up with a genuine reason for not
taking my money. We asked them to take £10,000. I had an account
with them and, although my limit was modest, they knew me well.

Eventually I threatened to object to their permit and they paid me out.' The only possible explanation that occurs to me for the Tote refusing Mr Nelson's bet is that, for PR reasons, they wanted to keep the ultimate dividend higher than the Starting Price. 'I tried to get on everywhere with everyone,' recalls Nelson, 'but only one hedging bookmaker, and Hill's – who took £8,000 – would accommodate me; and I've remembered that when doing business ever since.'

As the Tote is supposedly state-owned and exists to plough its profits back into horse racing, its operating methods are of interest to all racegoers. A senior official of the Tote was outraged that I should want to include this story in the book. Mr Nelson did indeed have an account, he said, but he hadn't used it for some eight years, and it was intended only for the hedging of Tote bets. He admitted they had 'paid him £1,000 to avoid going to court', suggesting that similar settlements were commonplace in the betting industry. If so, I am unaware of it.

Back in sunny Majorca, John Nelson stayed on the phone, at great expense to his office phone bill, to listen to the last race. His carefully cultivated tan was already beginning to fade!

In the Press Room at Ascot the hacks were hastily rewriting their stories and alerting their colleagues back in the newsrooms that a story of great import now needed space on the news pages. Brough Scott, for example, was there to write about the Queen Elizabeth II Stakes for the *Sunday Telegraph*: 'By the time I had written the piece and sent it, the tally was up to five. By the time I was making a check call, Frankie had put six on the reel and I was telling the office, "It can't happen because he is riding a 20/1 outsider which hasn't run for three months – but if he was to clock this race as well, you had better clear the decks . . .".'

While the telephone lines were buzzing from Canary Wharf to the Balearics, the man himself just had time to pop up to BBC TV's eyrie to talk to Julian Wilson – a firm clasp of hands and a breathless query from Frankie: 'Did Arsenal win?'

'2–0,' volunteered a nearby hack.

'*Yyess!* What a day!' cried the jockey. 'Don't touch me,' he warned Wilson, 'because I'm *red 'ot*! I'm definitely going to do the Lottery tonight! I've had some great days in my life,' he went on, 'but this will take all to beat [*sic*].' When asked about the one race remaining, he unwittingly gave the conspiracy theorists a stick with which to beat him later: 'I don't think this time the boys are going to let me win this one.'

'This is one of the most amazing days in the history of Ascot,' an unusually animated Wilson told viewers, before urging Dettori, 'Frankie – go out and do it!'

LOCHANGEL: Sire – Night Shift; out of – Peckitt's Hill.

RESULT: 1. Lochangel (Dettori) 5/4JF; 2. Corsini (P. Eddery) 5/4JF. 5 ran. Winning distance: ¾ length. Trainer: I. Balding. Tote win return: £2.70.

CHAPTER EIGHT

'NO MATTER HOW FAR YOU TRAVEL, OR HOW SMART YOU GET,' SAID
THE FATHER TO THE WOULD-BE PROFESSIONAL GAMBLER SON,
'ALWAYS REMEMBER THIS: SOMEDAY A GUY IS GOING TO COME UP
TO YOU AND SHOW YOU A NICE, BRAND NEW DECK OF CARDS ON
WHICH THE SEAL IS NEVER BROKEN, AND THIS GUY IS GOING TO
OFFER TO BET YOU THAT THE JACK OF SPADES WILL JUMP OUT OF THE
DECK AND SQUIRT CIDER IN YOUR EAR. SON, DO NOT BET HIM, FOR
AS SURE AS YOU DO, YOU'RE GOING TO GET AN EAR FULL OF CIDER'

DAMON RUNYON

'BY NOW YOU COULD SEE FEAR IN THE EYES OF THE RING
BOOKMAKERS'

MALCOLM HOWARD

NOW THE DAY HAD moved into the outer limits of
anyone's experience, an unknown zone where normal rules
no longer applied. Rob Hartnett's over-riding memory was of
the whole racecourse seeming 'in a state of disbelief' during the
build-up to this race. Racegoers knew they were on the brink of
witnessing an unprecedented, almost unimaginable achievement. No
hyperbole could match the magnitude of what could be just minutes
away. Punters were on the verge of winning small, and in a couple of
cases very substantial, fortunes. Because of the accumulator bets they
had taken, bookmakers off-course were launching the greatest damage
limitation exercise they had ever undertaken. For the on-course
bookmakers, many severely wounded already by repeated blows to the
satchel, financial catastrophe was staring them in the face should
Frankie win again. But should he lose, they also sensed one last opportunity of fighting off ruin.

Here was a surreal situation to which no one quite knew how to react. The well-understood and established rules of behaviour had flown out of the betting-shop windows, taken wing from the race-course betting rings, and certainly gone AWOL amongst punters used to a system that gave the initiative to the old enemy, the bookie. Now it was all coming down to instinct and how those in the thick of it all reacted in the heat of a very special moment.

The form book chances of Fujiyama Crest winning the final race were, inevitably, not the sole determinants of what the horse's price should be. What would take place now was like the defining argument in a long-running family feud between close but competitive twin brothers. On-course bookies have always felt they are much truer representatives of their trade than their flashier off-course relatives – who in turn have always begrudged the way layers at the track are able to influence the odds at which the shops must settle their bets. Here was the ideal situation for a stubborn stand-off. The on-course boys knew the off-course fellows were desperate for Frankie's horse to start at the shortest odds possible in order to limit their liabilities. But the track layers were aware that on the form book this horse would have his work cut out. In fact, he was unlikely to win.

Therefore, this horse was fully entitled to start at odds of around 12/1, but racegoers would be prepared to take a much shorter price because so many of them were merely playing up the earnings they'd already pocketed. The off-course reps were not only prepared to do the same, they positively wanted to see Fujiyama Crest start at odds-on. The first part of the equation was quite acceptable to the course layers. However, they felt strongly that they could both clean up and put their high street counterparts' noses out of joint by going so far with the odds, but no further – perhaps through pig-headedness, maybe sheer bravado.

'I remember that day very well,' one betting-shop assistant, who identified himself as 'Insider' on The Racing Forum website, told me – giving me a sense of the massive payouts even one single high-street shop was facing after Frankie's sixth horse had gone in. 'The biggest bet was a Lucky 63 staked for a 20p unit and had a return of just over £10,000. It wasn't until the third or fourth race that we really began to realize what was happening, and the number of multiple bets with the same horses. Needless to say, HQ and the bosses were shitting themselves, and it was not possible to get through to notify them of the huge liabilities on the sixth and seventh leg.'

In an effort to ensure that Frankie's final mount would start at long odds-on, and thus at least diminish the ultimate betting shop payout, their on-course representatives were now piling big-money bets onto the bookies in the ring. Yet, though on-course bookies have an unrivalled reputation in the wider world for hard-nosed scepticism, even cynicism, at Ascot from 5 p.m. that day they appeared to take, en masse, an illogical and fateful decision. Astonishingly, the on-course bookies decided to take everything the off-course bookies could throw at them.

PERHAPS NONE OF THEM stopped to recall other black days when the sympathetic favourites of the people had overcome all obstacles to win and public gambles had paid off. Think of Red Rum's third Grand National win; the emotional triumph of cancer victim Bob Champion and his injury-prone partner Aldaniti, also in the National; or the brave, battling victories of everyone's favourite grey horse, Desert Orchid. All these victories had inflicted monetary maulings on the men who call the odds.

Did none of their invariably suspicious minds turn back to the day when several times champion jump jockey Peter Scudamore cantered to victory at Ascot in his last ever race on well-backed 5/2 favourite Sweet Duke? Did they not recall how eyebrows were again raised when Declan Murphy came back triumphantly from a life-threatening fall? Had they forgotten how Walter Swinburn had celebrated his own return from serious injury with a winner? Could they not see that this afternoon had acquired a momentum of its own – that the tide of fate was running irresistibly in Frankie Dettori's favour?

Do you know, I don't believe they could. They were too busy raking in 'mug money' – bets being shovelled in their direction by people they dismissed as naive enough to believe that, because he'd ridden the last six winners, Frankie would automatically, inevitably, win the seventh.

There is an old racing adage that says, 'If you missed the wedding, don't go to the funeral.' On this occasion, with 'six weddings' to their credit already, most punters were eagerly hoping to consummate their day's winnings with a last race honeymoon. Similar advice suggesting that they should beware a last race catastrophe by slashing the odds was now being hurled at the on-course layers by the bookmakers' representatives – who were actually as eager to give them large sums as they were fervently hopeful of not having to return to collect the winnings.

BUT THERE IS A larger and infinitely more difficult issue to consider. Did the layers never stop to wonder if maybe, just maybe, when those stalls flew open for this seventh race, the will to win amongst Frankie's fellow jockeys might be less intense than usual? Might they even feel intimidated by the thought of winning this particular race – of beating him and thereby being the one who prevented history being made? Remember the opprobrium suffered by Doug Smith when he brought Gordon Richards' winning sequence to an end?

John Karter was for a long while a respected racing journalist at the *Sunday Times*, and is also the author of an unauthorized biography of Frankie Dettori. But he has since given up the racing life to qualify as a psychotherapist – a fascinating career change, which enables him to put himself inside the mind of a jockey walking out to take part in that final race. 'He might well be thinking, "What am I going to do if it comes to the last furlong and I'm in a position to challenge him?"' ponders Karter. 'I think that possibility may just take the edge off his challenge. I'm sure the significance of the race would be at the back of every other jockey's mind. I remember being at Cheltenham,' he continues, 'when Michael Dickinson saddled the first five in the Gold Cup. I was in the weighing room, savouring the atmosphere, when Jonjo O'Neill, who had only finished well down the field, came in, punching the air in excitement, shouting, "I was there", thrilled just to have been part of an historic event. Being a jockey in Frankie's last race that day would have felt like that.' John, who has no regrets at leaving behind the frequently incestuous and uncritical racing scene, stresses he is not implying anything untoward about the conduct of the last race – simply that the whole atmosphere and momentum of the situation must have played a part in the ultimate outcome.

Karter's diagnosis is corroborated by the authors of *In The Zone: Transcendent Experience In Sports*, a book (written before Dettori day) examining instances of abnormal sporting achievement. 'A winner's confidence,' Michael Murphy and Rhea A. White fascinatingly assert, 'can radiate like an aura and be a palpable threat to every competitor.' In detailing examples of extraordinary deeds achieved when the atmosphere must have been comparable with Ascot's – notably at the Olympics – they define the 'zone' itself as 'a psychological space in which one's performance seems supernormal. Sport has enormous power,' they continue, 'to sweep us beyond our ordinary sense of self, to evoke capacities that have generally been regarded as mystical, occult, or religious.' Mumbo-jumbo or a decent description of the lead-up to the 5.35 at Ascot?

I have developed a theory of my own about the frequency with which the sentimental outcome comes to pass in horse racing. Whether it is the first ride of a significant comeback, the last ride of an illustrious career or even the potential world-record seventh winner on an Ascot card, a kind of collective hysteria overcomes those involved. It is almost as though they succumb to what they perceive as the inevitable, or desirable, and therefore – subconsciously no doubt – permit it to happen, as it were, by default. It is the same kind of hysteria that will see one nervous child faint at a public function – to be swiftly followed by the rest of the class – or one person purporting to spot a UFO, followed frequently by a whole group of fellow spectators. You need a very strong personality to stand up to this kind of involuntary peer pressure.

Similar inevitabilities or outcomes preordained by the fates happen in other sports. Every football supporter knows about the player who returns to score against his old club even when his previous form has been abysmal. In the Tour de France, unheralded riders with a connection to the region in which a stage is finishing often manage to cross the line in front. The authors of *The Zone* quote the 1976 Olympic decathelete Bruce Jenner as saying, 'I was rising above myself, doing things I had no right to be doing.' Add in the overwhelming confidence radiating through Frankie, and you have a recipe for the hoped-for to become fact: a self-fulfilling prophecy – the world wanted Frankie to win, so win he would.

BY THIS POINT IN the day even a hard-nosed 'semi-professional' punter could see the effects of the mass psychosis that had taken hold. Malcolm Howard, the author of *How To Find Value* and other books about the concept of value betting, was firmly of the opinion that as Pat Eddery had proved he was riding well with second places on both Bosra Sham and Corsini, it just had to be his turn in the last race. But he admits, 'the atmosphere was electric, and the only thing on everyone's mind was: can Frankie go through the card? By now, you could see fear in the eyes of the ring bookmakers. They knew that Frankie's mount, Fujiyama Crest, could not possibly win the last race, but with liabilities mounting up on this jockey they were forced to bet to false odds. My analysis suggested that fair odds would have been: 4/1 Durham, 4/1 Northern Fleet, 6/1 Ivor's Flutter, 6/1 Flocheck, 9/1 Fujiyama Crest, 10/1 bar. The actual odds – 2/1 Fujiyama Crest, 9/2 Durham, 9/1 Northern Fleet, 10/1 bar – demonstrated to me that the bookmakers knew they would end up having a disastrous day, and in some cases they were betting to avoid bankruptcy by taking money for ANYTHING not ridden by Frankie.'

At 9/1, therefore, Eddery's mount represented such 'value' to Howard that he invested £50 to collect £500 after the race. 'I felt really smug. I was a semi-professional, rational punter when all around me were emotional lunatics throwing their money away on a moderate horse at shameful odds!'

Taking everything in with a bemused air was professional punter Alan Potts, author of *Against The Crowd*. The title of his best-selling guide to serious punting seems particularly appropriate to that Saturday afternoon. 'I feel privileged to have seen racing's biggest news story since L. Piggott inadvertently omitted two zeroes from his tax return,' says Potts. 'But it was distinctly galling for a hard-working professional punter to be surrounded by thousands of mugs, who were backing winner after winner without any more knowledge than a jockey's name. Equally, with so many smiling faces in the crowd it was impossible not to share their pleasure at a once-in-a-lifetime experience for punters.'

THE TIME-HONOURED BETTING system of 'tail wags the dog' was now undergoing its most rigorous and searching examination. At the head offices of the Big Three bookies – William Hill, Ladbrokes and Coral – the staggering financial implications of a final success for Frankie in the seventh race had well and truly sunk in. Twelve months earlier Fujiyama Crest had won this very same race starting at 8/1, but this Saturday morning, having run poorly recently and burdened with more weight this year, it had been freely offered at double-figure odds for a repeat performance.

The biggest course bet of the day, £30,000, had made an appearance when the price, which opened at 3/1, then drifted in places to 6/1 before collapsing to 6/4, had returned to 2/1, where it stayed, resisting all attempts to drive it lower. There were also four £20,000 wagers staked, another of £15,000, one of £12,000, four of £10,000, seven of £8,000, one of £7,000, half a dozen of £5,000, a couple more at £4,000, yet another of £3,000, ten of £2,000, two of £1,600 and one of £1,200.

Frantic efforts began to force down the odds. *Sporting Life* reporter Doug Newton logged details of 'known substantial bets' for Fujiyama Crest in the betting ring totalling almost £600,000. Why did the price refuse to drop any lower than 2/1?

This is what seems to have happened. The on-course men were certain that Fujiyama Crest would not win. On that basis, therefore, to be able to take virtually unlimited cash at 2/1 for what should on the form book have been a 12/1 shot, was a phenomenon so rare in their experience as to be unique. It was also, one might suggest, capable of clouding their business judgement, which would normally, one might have thought, have encouraged them to acquire the capital available at the lowest rate of liability. 'Common sense and experience went out of the window,' is how William Hill's long-serving course representative Mike Burton, one of the most senior bookmakers in the game, puts it: 'People believed their Klondike gold rush had come. Nothing that day made much sense – it will probably never happen again in the same way. People in a foreign situation like this will forget the rule book by which they would usually act. I'm still of the belief that there were some big layers who were not actively trading that day who saw what was happening and supported the market illegally – they couldn't resist laying bets through a figurehead or third party. They created a cesspit of intrigue, which will never be unravelled. The ring became lopsided like never before. Bookmakers were chasing money – it made gamblers out of them. They couldn't resist it, their heads caught fire. They thought they'd found the gold at the end of the rainbow – but it was fools' gold.'

Neal Wilkins, the Press Association's Chief Starting Price Reporter, with a quarter of a century's experience behind him, declared that he had, 'never seen so much betting activity before as for that final race – even at Royal Ascot or the Cheltenham Festival meetings. The bookies chose to stand the horse at 3/1 – that was the general opening price. They felt they had to take it on. The office agents were knocking each other over, but the course bookies were standing their ground, feeling the horse couldn't possibly win. In the past the off-course bookmakers, particularly Ladbrokes, had had things their own way, but this time the bookies wouldn't be bullied into shortening the odds. They didn't know the enormity of the off-course liabilities, but perhaps those firms should have sent still more money down.'

One on-course layer, very much in the minority, had an inkling of what was laying in wait for him. 'The mood in the betting ring just before the last race,' Alan Potts recalled, 'was summed up by the appeal from one Tatts bookmaker, who pleaded with me, "Al, this can't win, can it? It can't win?"'

Let us hear from one such on-course layer: the opinionated, flamboyant Barry Dennis, who survived the experience to go on, ironically, to become infamous for 'Barry's Bismarcks' on Channel 4's *Morning Line* show – fancied horses he tipped to lose. 'For me to be able to lay 2/1 about a 10/1 shot is massive value that we don't get the chance to exploit very often,' he explains. 'We were open-mouthed, gobsmacked. It can never happen again in our lifetime. I didn't bother squaring the books. I stood the bets and lost heavily. The prices laid about Fujiyama Crest represent laying 4/1 about the correct roulette number, which is a 35/1 chance. The odds against Frankie riding seven in a row are the same as against me beating Stephen Hendry in a snooker match. For me to be able to lay 7/4 against that happening on the last race, I've got to lay it to more money than I can afford to lose because it was tremendous value.'

Fellow layer Gary Wiltshire concurs: 'I was laying 2/1 about a horse I made a 10/1 chance at least. The odds were miles wrong. I laid all comers. I would do it again tomorrow.' Even a colleague who wasn't there agreed – Bristol bookie Andy Smith, who was forced by traffic delays on the M32 to go to Worcester racetrack instead. 'I would have done my brains at Ascot. At the prices involved I would have laid Frankie's last winner all day and night.'

The bookies were about to cop an earful of cider.

CHAPTER NINE

'WHEN GOD IS MOVING IN ONE OF HIS MYSTERIOUS WAYS, NOT
EVEN THE FORM BOOK IS LIKELY TO PREVAIL'

PROFESSIONAL GAMBLER ALAN POTTS

WITH THE POSSIBILITY OF history being made, BBC
Television now had another big decision to make. 'We
transmitted the fifth and sixth races live,' recalled Julian
Wilson, 'but to cover the seventh live would have disrupted
BBC1's evening schedules. Presentation vetoed it. I asked them
to show it. They said no.' You could see Presentation's point: live
coverage of the last race would have meant the cancellation of a
much-repeated episode of *Dad's Army*, 'The Making of Private Pike',
due to precede the *Generation Game* at 5.35 p.m. 'It was a fuck-up, to
be honest,' reflects Wilson. 'I had a go at them, but they are rather
like the Jockey Club – not the sort of people who ever say sorry. A
shame . . .'.

After Decorated Hero's victory, however, BBC Radio had taken a
very timely decision, which took its veteran racing correspondent
Peter Bromley (who retired from the Corporation after giving his
final commentary on the Derby in 2001) very much by surprise.
'They'd been unimpressed when I'd pointed out what was happening
in the previous couple of races,' he remembers, 'but finally accepted
that this was an occasion demanding live coverage.' At the last possible minute he was told they were taking a live feed into the Radio 5
Live *Sports Report* show – normally devoted to football at this time in
the afternoon. It left him, he reflects, 'totally and absolutely unprepared to call the race'.

Meanwhile, word about the extraordinary happenings at
Ascot was spreading rapidly around the globe, courtesy of bearded,

well-upholstered journalist and broadcaster Christopher Poole, who was already feeling as though he'd backed a string of winners. He was broadcasting, as he had done for years, for the BBC World Series *Sports World* programme, which has an audience of up to 30 million each week, in twenty-six countries. That day they'd set out to broadcast the first three races, but after each Dettori victory his producer had said, 'We'll have to do another one . . .'. 'This was music to my ears,' says Chris, 'as my somewhat unusual contract stipulated that I was paid by the minute. So for every extra piece I did I was coining it in! Frankie did me very well that day, even though I didn't back any of his winners.' (Chris obviously had a better agent than John Hanmer – whose additional fee for 'overtime' that afternoon was the same regardless of how much extra work was involved.)

With BBC TV having opted out of showing the last so that Captain Mainwaring could strut his stuff, anyone wishing to see the race live had to head for their local betting shop. Satellite Information Services, who provide this broadcast coverage, were also transmitting live to a wide range of foreign countries – Austria, Belgium, Bulgaria, the Canary Islands, Cyprus, the Czech Republic, Denmark, France, Germany, Gibraltar, Greece, Italy, Malta, Netherlands, Norway, Poland, Portugal, Romania, the Spanish mainland, Sweden and the Caribbean. In the majority of these countries the race was also being shown in their equivalent of betting shops, at racecourses, in casinos and other commercial outlets. A number of American racecourses also took the live pictures for racegoers to watch while awaiting the action at their own track.

FUJIYAMA'S STABLE LAD DEREK Heeney, you may recall, had asked his wife to put a bet on for him on his charge. Earlier in the day, therefore, she had stuck her head round the door of their local Newmarket betting shop to see what price was on offer. She'd been told it was available at 16/1. She went off to finish the shopping. On her return she was somewhat taken aback to discover that those odds were now shown at 15/8. At such cramped odds she decided not to bother backing the horse.

APPROPRIATELY ENOUGH, GIVEN THAT Frankie Dettori had been well and truly in the pink all afternoon, he came out for the last race wearing plenty of it in the silks of Fujiyama Crest's owner, Mr Seisuke Hata. The jacket was royal blue, with a pink triple diamond, the cap pink with a royal blue diamond.

Trained by Michael Stoute, Frankie's four-year-old mount, a bay gelding bred in the USA by Roi Danzig out of Snoozy Time, was wearing a visor, as he had done before. Something of a cross between blinkers and a hood, which keeps the ears uncovered but offers more of a mask than a set of blinkers, it is designed to keep a horse's mind on the job in hand by preventing his eyes from looking from side to side.

The final race was the Class C Gordon Carter Handicap, with £20,000 added to stakes, over a lengthy trip of 2 miles 45 yards. Fujiyama Crest had triumphed twelve months ago in the same race when he had been an 8/1 shot. Amongst his fifteen rivals had been a well backed 5/2 favourite, Istabraq, ridden by Willie Carson, who could only manage eleventh place. The horse's true calling would only emerge when he was put over hurdles, and went on to run up a sequence of Champion Hurdle victories in 1998, 1999 and 2000. Drawn ten that day, Frankie and Fujiyama had made virtually all the running before going clear in the final quarter of a mile to win by three lengths. The first prize of £14,525 had rounded off a hugely successful season that had seen the horse win five times. Sir Michael Stoute – a man so focused on flat racing that he rang me to talk about Dettori when the Grand National meeting was on the box – believed he had Fujiyama in good shape, and had no doubt about the gameplan: 'Frankie was always going to make the running.'

Nevertheless, last time out Fujiyama Crest had been tailed off in the Northumberland Plate at Newcastle and, in contrast to the modest 8st. 8lbs he had been set to carry a year ago, today he had to heft 9st. 10lbs. It was the heaviest burden carried by any of the eighteen runners, and consequently there was some discussion amongst racegoers and betting shop patrons about the race tactics Frankie – who also felt his mount had a stone too much weight – might adopt. His horse's best form had invariably been achieved when making the running, but, with two or three others in the field who had also demonstrated their best performances when allowed to bowl along in front, the crowd was waiting with bated breath to discover what would happen as the stalls opened.

Prior to all this, however, it turns out that Julian Wilson had nearly prevented Fujiyama Crest from running any more flat races at all. Acting as selling agent for the horse, he'd come close to striking a deal with leading National Hunt trainer Martin Pipe. 'I'd told him I thought this might be the horse for him,' explains Wilson – one of the few people I know who can boast Bonhote amongst their middle names – 'that the horse had the size and scope to make a jumper, and that he could buy him for £60,000.' Fortunately for Frankie Dettori and everyone else, ultimately Pipe didn't take Wilson's advice. Indeed, Wilson, who fancied Fujiyama for the last, didn't take his own advice – neglecting to back the horse. But, as Brough Scott pointed out, 'Fujiyama Crest looked an unlikely accomplice for the Hall of Fame.'

Amongst the horse's opponents was a three-year-old gelding called Shooting Light, ridden by Tim Sprake. At 33/1 it was the longest priced runner in the field – unsurprisingly perhaps, since the Ascot racecard was noting it 'possibly stays 14 furlongs' – hardly the best recommendation in a 16-furlong race. The horse's owners were Michael Blackburn and J.M. Brown – the same John Brown who was boss of bookies William Hill, just about to take one almighty hit courtesy of Frankie Dettori. John insists he was joking when he gave Sprake his riding instructions: 'If you can get anywhere near Frankie, stick him over the rails – I'll pay your fine.'

BEFORE THEY HAD COME out, fellow jockey Walter Swinburn, who was on the 14/1 chance Embryonic, had told Frankie, 'You'll never get this close again.'

'If it happens, it happens,' the Italian insisted. 'If it doesn't, it's been a fantastic day anyhow.'

Most of the other jockeys were stood outside the weighing room on the steps. Walking out now, besieged by autograph hunters and well-wishers – even, remembers fellow-jockey Ray Cochrane, who was riding the 16/1 chance Pike Creek, also trained by Ian Balding, people trying to kiss him – Dettori still managed to take in that the approximate odds board was displaying odds of just 2/1 on his part-ner – when earlier they had been 12/1. 'If I'd known there was £25 or £30 million involved, I might have panicked and done something wrong,' he later suggested – though for a man who had already won nearly £400,000 of prize money for the owners of his six winners that afternoon, this sounds a little unlikely.

Before this final race the barely-restrained excitement at Ascot was palpable. 'With the finale set to commence from stalls in front of the stands,' wrote J.A. McGrath, the course commentator that day, in the *Daily Telegraph* subsequently, 'it was as if the occasion had been stage managed.' The crowd, four deep on the rails, cheered and clapped Dettori as he cantered Fujiyama Crest up the straight to the starting point. 'The applause was as warm and spontaneous as any I have heard on a racecourse anywhere.' 'You could feel the high-voltage buzz running through the crowd,' agrees his press room colleague Jonathan Powell. 'Many of us felt we were on the verge of witnessing a defining sporting achievement.'

Drawn in stall one, Frankie was nearest to the stand side and to the left of Ray Cochrane. As the jockeys waited for all the horses to be stalled, Cochrane turned to ask Frankie what he would be doing – sit-ting in? up there? dropping out? 'Before I could get the words out – "I'm rockin', mate, rockin' – making it." Oh, yeah? I thought, uh-oh. Making it round here, with a lot of others doing the same – you could come unstuck here, mate. Two mile handicaps at Ascot can be very rough races sometimes – well, most times, really – especially down near Swinley Bottom.' But as the stalls sprung open just one minute later than the scheduled off time of 5.35, Frankie headed smartly for the front of the field. 'He was gone,' says Ray Cochrane, 'backside in the saddle, driving up to the pace. He was making it, going a great clip, too.' Soon Frankie found himself in front, with no other jockey in these early stages seeming particularly keen to take him on. Cochrane, in his usual place somewhere near the back, was not worried – they were going a gallop and 'with a bit of luck they would cut each other's throats and I might sneak up on them'.

KEVIN DARLEY, REIGNING CHAMPION jockey at the time, was on Ian Balding's other runner in the race, Paul Mellon's four-year-old Silently, a 25/1 shot. 'You never know what to expect in these competitive handicaps at Ascot over this trip,' he says. 'The first thing in every jockey's mind is to get your position and hope for a clear passage through the race. If you have the horse and you know he stays then the best place to be to stay out of trouble is in front. Frankie didn't want any hard luck stories after the exceptional day he'd had, and obviously had the run of the race in front.'

Peter Bromley had begun his radio commentary. 'I had done no homework on the race,' he emphasises, 'as there had been no plans to cover it. I only reached the commentary position when the runners were milling round at the start – and even when they were half way round I didn't really know who half of them were. Fortunately, though, it didn't really matter, as I could identify Frankie easily enough – and he was the story.' (Anyone wishing to check out the accuracy of Peter's commentary should ring Ascot racecourse and ask to be put on hold – whereupon they will then hear his exciting report of the closing stages, with specially composed music adding to the stirring effect.)

By now, 5 Live racing correspondent Cornelius Lysaght, away at a colleague's wedding, had been persuaded that the wild rumour of Frankie Dettori going through the card at Ascot was true. 'History was in danger of being made. I recall listening to 5 Live's commentary on race seven with a mixture of envy for not being there, and concern that I would never be allowed a day off again.'

'Frankie took the race by the scruff of the neck,' wrote J.A. McGrath, describing the jockey's tactics as 'a magnificent display of judging pace from the front'. It looked as though the other serious contenders were content to play a waiting game and save their challenges for later. Passing the winning post for the first time very early on, the field began to turn right-handed round the first bend, and Frankie took the first of several swift glances behind to determine who might be on his heels.

Down the runners went to Swinley Bottom. 'It was then,' remembers Cochrane, 'when we heard the noise. It was the crowd in the stands roaring.' Although Frankie swung his horse wide of the running rail, leaving an appreciable gap on his inside, neither Pat Eddery on the chasing Northern Fleet nor the apprentice Paul Doe on Meant To Be – who had finished fourth in the race the previous season – wanted to put the leader under pressure at this stage. Cochrane moved through some tiring horses, but the leader was in a great rhythm, just galloping along. Frankie pressed ahead as the watching hordes wondered when a significant attempt to take him on would materialise. With 5 furlongs to run, he felt Fujiyama was still 'pretty fresh' and 'not dying on me'.

'The dream was starting to unfold before our eyes,' continued McGrath. Stable lad Derek Heeney was already confidently telling anyone who cared to listen, 'He's won!' and mentally calculating the winnings coming to him from the bet he'd told his wife to put on.

There was about half a mile to run, and now Pat Eddery decided to galvanize Northern Fleet, on whom, he later told me, he thought he had a great chance. Eddery began to close on Fujiyama Crest who, in turn, was reminded of his responsibilities by a jockey now putting all thoughts of post-race celebrations out of his mind. 'I asked him for the effort,' Frankie was to recall, 'he responded, and started to stretch.' Northern Fleet had now cut the lead to an agonisingly narrow margin, and was still closing; Miroswaki and Seb Sanders had charged through behind the two principals to get to within a couple of lengths of them. The rest of the field, says Ray Cochrane, 'had either run out of petrol or got a flat tyre'. Now it was 'just Pat and Frankie, hammer and tongs all the way up the straight', with Fujiyama Crest 100 per cent committed to holding on. 'They're into the last furlong, and I don't think you'll hear a word I'm saying,' bellowed Peter Bromley to riveted radio listeners, 'because you'll realize that Fujiyama Crest and Frankie Dettori have the lead, but Northern Fleet is going after him . . .'.

'I could hear the crowd,' remembered Frankie, 'it was a persistent roar.' Brough Scott defines it as 'a tone that brooked no other answer'. 'I could swear that the noise literally carried the horse to the line,' says Clare Balding. Timeform's Jim McGrath recalls Ladbroke's Mike Dillon 'screaming for Pat Eddery'. Ray Cochrane says the noise was unbelievable. Let Frankie Dettori talk us through the final yards:

> I could feel Fujiyama getting tired – the weight was beginning to tell. I could see this horse appearing, and I could hear him – Pat at his very best, going all out, really going for it. I was just praying to God – please, winning post, come. Old Fujiyama was so tired and just managed to get there on the line. I just punched the air and I was that exhausted I nearly fell off.

Frankie had done it. Seven up. History made. A legend launched. A reputation committed to posterity.

At that precise moment the clock in one of bookie John Nelson's North London betting shops stopped dead. 'I've left it ever since – I call it Dettori time.'

Up in Scotland at the Broughty Ferry branch of William Hill that Alan McEwen was managing, the shop had been packed by the time of the last race, and even the cashiers knew Frankie's colours. 'Many of our customers are professional people,' Alan told me, 'and unlike some betting shops, it is rare to hear them roar like a football crowd. But as he came home in the last, the noise from my branch must have hit the street outside. The hairs on the back of my neck still stand up when I think back.'

Fred Done had now discovered that he had lost £1.5 million. 'I was very happy' was, unexpectedly, his reaction. 'At last I knew what we owed, and I knew that we could live with it and settle, we were still in the game.' 'Logic said that history was beyond us,' says Brough Scott, 'but instinct told us that it would happen.' He got straight on the phone to the *Sunday Telegraph*'s news desk, 'and was able, for at least this once, to utter the immortal phrase, "Hold the front page!"'

Even though *Grandstand* was now off the air, at BBC Television Centre pictures were still coming in. 'The studio was cheering as much as I was,' says soccer statistician Albert Sewell, whose two bets containing all seven Dettori winners had now come good – for a stake of £5, he now had over £500 to collect. 'For weeks after I was asked why I hadn't backed Frankie's seven in a roll-up. The answer was simple – I'd never given it a thought. It had never been done before, so why should it happen that day?'

As Frankie cantered back, Ray Cochrane heard Pat Eddery say, 'I had him beat, but I just could not get by him.'

THE CONTRAST BETWEEN THE celebrating racegoers and the stunned bookies was stark. The layers felt just like the poker player who sits confidently with four kings in his hand, betting against an inscrutable opponent who doesn't even bother to look at his cards before triumphantly turning up four aces. 'My clerk Peter Houghton was absolutely stunned,' says Gary Wiltshire. 'He just stood there, gripping the book and staring into space. I had to punch him quite hard to bring him back.' Wiltshire was facing a loss of £800,000. 'The mountainous Mr Wiltshire looked like he had received a direct hit from a torpedo,' the *Guardian*'s Jamie Reid told me. 'It was like watching a huge balloon deflating rapidly.' Wiltshire's clerk wasn't the only one struck dumb. Neal Wilkins of the Press Association was watching the faces of the layers. 'They looked physically drained. They took it on the chin even though they knew just what it was costing.'

AS DETTORI AND FUJIYAMA Crest walked back deliberately slowly to savour the moment, Frankie was congratulated by his fellow riders – 'even they were shell-shocked'. John Reid shook his hand; Simon

Whitworth slapped his hand extravagantly; Jason Weaver rode over to grab Frankie's hand as the Italian wrapped an arm around his shoulders. He came into the enclosure and the enormous crowd closed behind him just like the spectators following the last-day Open leader at the eighteenth. 'It was the sea of history breaking over him,' observed Brough Scott. Frankie asked Dave, his valet, and Ascot's PR man, Alistair Haggis, to fetch from the weighing room the bottle of champagne he'd received after the previous race so that he could celebrate *à la* Michael Schumacher!

Beaming delightedly, and blowing kisses to the throng of spectators, Frankie crouched low to embrace Fujiyama Crest's perspiring neck, then hurled himself aloft in probably his highest ever celebration leap, to land lightly on his feet, drop his whip, and fling his arms around John Ferguson, the horse's manager. He got a big hug from trainer Michael Stoute, laughing perhaps with relief that he hadn't let the side, and crowd, down – or perhaps because Frankie had just said to him, 'It musta been the two Weetabixes I had for breakfast!'

'I'm just warming up – is there any more racing?' shouted the exuberant Italian, who was now almost beside himself with the sheer thrill of the occasion. Someone called for three cheers, vigorously '*Hurrah*'ed by the ecstatic crowd, the vast majority of whom were smiling for England – and Italy. 'E'en the ranks of Tuscany – in this case, the bookmakers – could scarce forbear to cheer,' quoted the erudite *Independent on Sunday* reporter, Sue Montgomery.

Now Geoff Lester of the *Sporting Life* – a man who had twice been through the card himself, at Newcastle and Ayr, albeit as a tipster, was due to take the microphone and interview Frankie in the winner's enclosure on behalf of the Ascot Executive. But he remembers what happened before that. 'The roars as he held off Pat in a thrilling finish were quite remarkable, but what followed was even more remarkable. There was a stampede from Tatts to get to the winner's enclosure – and that is a long sprint – and Frankie milked the occasion fully.' Having hurled his goggles into the crowd, Frankie had shaken up the champers and dashed wildly up and down the crowd, spraying it here, there and everywhere. 'I remember my wife Deirdre panicking on behalf of all the well-dressed ladies,' says the trainer Mark Johnston – before the jockey stopped for a well-deserved swig himself.

One lady whose evasive action proved ineffective was Maggie Emm, Ascot's Members Enclosure Manager, who was showered with bubbly, as was racegoer and SP reporter, David Smalley, for whom the experience was 'almost a privilege'. There was plenty flying into glasses in other parts of the course as well – champagne sales were later reported to have hit record levels.

'I decided to go for it from the first bell,' Frankie told Geoff. 'If they nailed me then so be it, but at least I was determined to make them do the running.' Off he went for the compulsory ritual of weighing in, to check that his weight in the race had been correct. 'In the underground quiet of the weighing room, he sat momentarily on the scales,' observed Brough Scott, 'then whooped off round bemused officials to jump into the arms of his old friend and valet Dave Currie.'

As the Judge at Ascot that day, Jonathan Dimsdale was in a privileged position to observe what happened. 'As the afternoon wore on, the atmosphere in the weighing room became more and more electric. When the last race took place, it almost seemed that all the other jockeys were just going to let Frankie get his seven – all, that is, except for Pat Eddery, who wasn't going to let anything like a new record come between him and a win. I found it very hard to announce the result,' he admits, 'and I suspect that the announcement was rather over the top.'

Back in the weighing room there was also plenty of bubbly floating around; everybody was in great heart. 'After we showered and Frankie came in to get changed, there was a big crowd of jocks in our corner,' says Ray Cochrane, 'all taking the mick and having some great craic, reflecting back on the day. One asked, had he really fancied all his rides? As he dashed off to the showers naked, glass of bubbly in one hand, towel in the other, he shouted, "No, I only fancied the one in the third!"' With the press milling around the weighing room, Kevin

Darley grabbed a photographer's camera and got an excellent shot of Frankie cooling down in the showers. Had he been in the position to beat the winner, Darley told me later, then the only thing on his mind would have been to win the race – but any jockey who denied Frankie his final winner, he added, 'would have been the most unpopular figure at Ascot, and certainly would have needed an escort from the track'. Later that evening Ray Cochrane wrote a small inscription above Frankie's dressing room peg, 'which I hope will be there for a long time. It was written by a mere mortal jock about a great day, a great achievement and about doing things most of us dream about.'

With the crowd in no mood to disperse, even though the bars on the course closed half an hour after the last race, Frankie appeared on the balcony of the grandstand, looking for all the world like a young Pope blessing an enthusiastic horde of dedicated believers.

MEDIA FRENZY WAS STILL building, with TV news crews arriving at the course having missed the actual racing, but hungry to interview anyone remotely connected with Frankie, or with a winning bet story to tell. 'The one really strong memory I have,' says Jonathan Dimsdale, 'is of Frankie being interviewed in the weighing room by BBC Radio just before he went home. He was clearly hyper, and understandably on cloud nine, but he gave the most lucid interview, and remembered to give racing a plug by saying that people should come racing to get the atmosphere. I thought such professionalism quite remarkable in the circumstances, and it completed my admiration of the man.'

Eventually it was time for Frankie to leave Ascot, but even then, to judge from this little anecdote told by racegoer Amanda Johnson, he was still on a high. After the seventh race Amanda had rushed to the paddock with the multitudes to try and get his autograph, but he was so overwhelmed with people that she decided to leave it. They'd stayed on in the hospitality box where they were being entertained for quite a while, and when they finally went to find their car they happened to see, near the Paddock, Frankie leaving at the same time. 'I thought he might be fed up with signing autographs,' says Amanda, 'and there were still people mobbing him, but I approached him and asked. I handed him my racecard, expecting him to sign the outside, but he said, "No, we must do it properly", and turned to the feature race, turned it the right way up and signed across his horse's name, Mark of Esteem. I thought that was a really nice touch, as he must have signed hundreds of autographs prior to this.' He had indeed – including one to Paul Haigh of the *Racing Post*, who is unrepentant about his most uncharacteristic lapse into sentimentality: 'When a man achieves the impossible and you're close enough to ask, you have to forget you're a grown-up who shouldn't bother with silly mementoes.'

Another racegoer, Jimmie Yardley from South London, who had taken his infant son Jamie to Ascot – and ended up spending most of the afternoon placating the unhappy baby – had spotted Frankie just a little earlier than Amanda. 'In its mysterious way,' he says, 'the day changed many people's lives in major and minor ways, and gave many people memories. My own favourite recollection is of seeing Frankie standing on a balcony of the grandstand, overlooking the winner's enclosure in the falling evening darkness, soaking up the atmosphere quietly after the crowds had gone. I had not gambled a penny that day, seen only one of the seven races, but I will be able to tell my son in years to come that he was there the day Frankie Dettori went through the card at Ascot.'

FUJIYAMA CREST: Sire – Roi Danzig; out of – Snoozy Time.
RESULT: 1. Fujiyama Crest (Dettori) 2/1; 2. Northern Fleet (P. Eddery) 9/1; 3. Miroswaki (S. Sanders) 12/1. Winning distance: neck, 2 lengths. Trainer: M. Stoute. Tote win return: £3.60.

CHAPTER TEN

'SATURDAY DEMONSTRATED BEYOND DOUBT WHAT EXCEPTIONAL
VALUE A BET IS. FOR A FEW POUNDS, PUNTERS WERE ABLE TO
WATCH HISTORY MADE, TO SAVOUR A TRULY REMARKABLE
MOMENT. BY COMPARISON, THE LOTTERY, OVER IN TWO MINUTES,
IS MEDIOCRE'

BBOA Chairman, Warwick Bartlett

FRANKIE DETTORI REMEMBERS RECEIVING more good-will wishes that evening 'than Bill Clinton when he became President'. Among the congratulatory calls was one from his father Gianfranco, who'd been following his son's progress during the afternoon on his television text service – and had told his wife there must be a fault because it kept putting up Frankie's name as winner of each race. At 9 p.m. his Magnificent Seven made third lead on the BBC's evening news, 'just after the war in Israel – probably the closest I can get to the main item!'

For others elsewhere, all over the country, the day was also coming to a memorable close. At the Freeman Hospital in Newcastle, staff had by now become a little concerned. It was already 5.45, and time for the evening meal, but their wheelchair-bound patient Harriet May Ion had still not returned from her afternoon out. Her son Raymond has a little explaining to do. 'I'd begun watching the racing, and kept meaning to take Mum back after each race. But, having been a racing man for thirty years, as Frankie continued winning I had to stay to see the outcome. I couldn't miss out on a day like this!' Raymond ended up having to watch the last race from a betting shop – which meant his mum's return to hospital got somewhat delayed. 'For all their virtues,' wonders Raymond, 'NHS staff seem to be one of the least racing-aware of professions! The doctors and nurses just didn't understand when I tried to explain why Mum and I were late.'

Derek Heeney, meanwhile, arrived home to be greeted by a shame-faced wife. She broke the news to him: because of the collapsing odds, she hadn't placed his bet. 'It would have been nice to win a few quid,' says the forgiving Derek, 'but being part of history made up for it – that was a great night.'

Up in the Morecambe branch of William Hill, where Darren Yates had placed his bet, 'there was a mixture of semi-panic and disbelief,' says manager Eddie Gough. 'I've never seen anything like it. After the seventh race, Darren came in – he appeared to be calm and collected. I don't know how.' Yates asked the counter clerk how much he'd won, 'thinking,' he admits, 'it would be about £50,000. When she told me it was half a million, I almost fainted.' (I wasn't hugely surprised to hear this. Working in betting shops myself for many years, I soon came to understand that few punters ever know precisely how much they have won – oddly enough, they frequently think it's rather less than they eventually receive!) Darren went to bed that night with his betting slip under his pillow, but he and his wife Annaley couldn't sleep, so they got up to plan how to spend their winnings. They'd only moved into their terraced house the previous Thursday – but a new home was still top of the list.

John Bolton returned from Ascot to London by train, listening to everyone talking excitedly about Dettori, and knowing he had a betting slip worth a fortune to cash. He and his wife Mary had already booked to dine that evening at one of London's best known restaurants, Langan's – 'but we couldn't really enjoy the meal for wondering about how much we had won,' admits Mary. Just to prove my earlier point, John reckoned it was about £300,000.

Back at Ascot, racing writer John Karter was completing his article for the next day's *Sunday Times*. Chris Poole of the BBC World Service plus a number of other journalists and racing figures were holding an impromptu drinks party in the Ascot car park. 'It was certainly the most exciting day I had had in forty years as a professional broadcast journalist,' says Poole. In due course Frankie Dettori, who was particularly well disposed towards the World Service because it broadcast to his native Italy, gave him an excellent interview. When John Karter finished his piece, however, he found that everyone else seemed to have cleared off and left him locked in the Press Room, so had to do a spot of balcony-climbing to break out – only to bump into Ascot's managing director, who promptly invited him home for supper!

Coral's PR man Rob Hartnett spent a busy evening 'being soaked with champagne, conducting a seemingly endless cycle of print, radio and TV interviews and all the time not having any real indication as to how much we had lost'.

Simon Clare is now a Public Relations executive for Coral Eurobet, but on this Saturday he was still finding his feet just one month into a more lowly role with Ladbrokes – 'a novice,' he freely admits. 'I certainly had not got used to working for a bookie after four years on the other side of the fence, working at the British Horseracing Board.' That day he was off duty, playing football for Carshalton against the Natwest Bank at Norbury, and oblivious to the dramas at Ascot. 'After the match I phoned my colleague Ed Nicholson, who had been on call, and he immediately shouted excitedly – he was always in a state of high excitement – down the phone, "Dettori has ridden all seven winners at Ascot!" I could not hide my delight. "Fantastic, wonderful – what a great achievement. This is unbelievable . . .". "What are you talking about, you idiot!" said Ed, shattering my innocence. "It's cost us millions of pounds! Our bonuses are out the window!"'

At the offices of the *Sporting Life*, they'd never changed a front page so many times during the course of one afternoon. Now, with a 7.40 p.m. deadline for Sunday's edition, acting editor Ben Newton was wrestling with headlines. 'Seventh Heaven' or 'Magnificent Seven'? 'We plumped for the latter.' Great minds think alike, for so did its rival the *Racing Post* in their first edition.

'I remember it as one of the most exciting nights of my career,' declared Jeremy Chapman, who was working alongside Newton, 'along with Lester getting three years for tax fraud and Dessie winning the Gold Cup. AND we came out on time, with one of the greatest front pages in the paper's history.' Though absent from the office, Tom Clarke, the editor, suggested making a poster of the front page available to readers at £1 per copy – and subsequently had a framed copy presented to Frankie Dettori at Ascot.

Alan Byrne, the *Racing Post*'s editor, still regrets not having been at Ascot himself. 'While there was something special about being in the office on the big day, the part of you that is a racing fan wants to be at the actual meeting.' For him the afternoon 'unfolded in a surreal way. After three or four races I realized we must have Frankie on the front page and we watched with amazement and slight horror as he went to five and six – we knew the implications for us.' Everybody gathered round the TV for the last race, spellbound – 'it seemed destined to happen, as if it was meant to be' – and then it became an 'absolute scramble' to get the first edition out. For the Monday paper the *Post* produced a Dettori poster across their centre spread.

'It has been a horrendous day,' said rails bookmakers Reeds, while a spokesman for Lewis Mendoza observed: 'Every bookmaker in the ring has had a terrible day. If a bookmaker hasn't lost a fortune this afternoon, then they just don't lay horses properly.'

On-course bookmaker Gary Wiltshire, however, knew he was facing ruin – up to £800,000 in liabilities. Normally he dined out at an Italian restaurant after a race meeting; tonight all he could face was fish and chips. Nevertheless, that evening he pulled himself together enough to turn up at Milton Keynes dog track to take bets and to watch Danny's Birthday, owned jointly with his son, run third. 'The first bet I took was a pound,' he says. 'I was thinking it was going to be a long way back from there.'

THE MOST PRECIOUS SOUVENIR I possess associated with the Magnificent Seven is the programme for the Division Two football match on 28 September 1996 between Luton Town and Blackpool. A confirmed Hatters fan and season ticket holder, I was therefore at Kenilworth Road, Luton that afternoon at 3.16 p.m. when – seven minutes before they came under orders for the Queen Elizabeth II Stakes – Luton 'striker' (I use the inverted commas intentionally) Kim Grant put the ball in the Blackpool net for the only goal of the game.

As usual, afterwards I set off home down the M1, and rang in to the office to check out the latest Premiership title betting, which I always distribute to the media on a Saturday evening. 'By the way,' I was told, 'Frankie Dettori has ridden all seven winners at Ascot.'

'Yes, and I've just had to take evasive action to avoid hitting a pink pig hovering above the motorway.'

I knew then that the journalists would gorge on a story involving big money wins and bookmaker misery, and that I was likely to be busy with press enquiries that evening. The first arrived even before I got home.

Once I got in, I checked with William Hill's Raceroom in Leeds for an idea of the scale of the financial damage inflicted on us. They were in turmoil and only able to tell me about the bets that had resulted in six figure returns. The four and five figure payouts were far too many to count. Fears were growing that this could be the worst day's trading the company – indeed the betting industry – had ever known. At this stage my information was that we were looking at a £5 million loss. Then I was informed of a bet placed in Morecambe in Lancashire, which had involved all of Frankie's winners, and smashed through the company's £500,000 payout limit by another 50-odd thousand.

This was the bet I decided to concentrate on. All I knew at this point was the make up of the bet and where it had been placed. I had no idea whose bet it was. A call to the shop in Morecambe supplied a name, but – since we never publicize winners' personal details without permission – I really needed to get hold of the customer to see if he would play ball with what I wanted to arrange. My priority was to make sure that when the media wrote and broadcast about betting on the day, they mentioned William Hill – we had at least to get some PR feedback even if by Monday there might not be a company to work for! To buy a little time, I put out a press release containing details of a 'Mystery Punter' who, thanks to Frankie Dettori, was half a million quid better off.

SURE ENOUGH, THE STORY dominated the Sunday papers. The headlines really went to town: 'Bookie Buster' (*Sunday Express*), 'Seven-up Dettori' (*Sunday Mirror*), 'Seven Steps to Immortality' (*Independent on Sunday*), 'Dettori is in 7th Heaven' (*Observer*), and 'Magnificent 7' (*Sunday Times, Mail on Sunday, Sunday Post*). 'The sequence will have cost the industry millions,' my colleague David Hood, William Hill's racing PR man, was quoted as saying. 'Three winners was expensive; four was dismal; five was appalling. When the last two went in, we turned off all the lights in Head Office.' On the Monday the *Daily Star* even addressed the occasion in its leader article – with a lesson it invited Tony Blair, then Prime Minister-in-waiting and about to address the annual Labour Party conference – to draw from the achievement:

Neigh Bother for Frankie

Salute our Gold Star hero today. He's a true punters' pal.

No, we don't mean Tony Blair on the eve of a Labour conference that could give him his toughest ride to date.

Hail super-jockey Frankie Dettori, whose seven scintillating wins on the trot created two half-millionaires and bashed the bookies where it REALLY hurts. Frankie, you're pure gold.

And Tony? It's one thing showing promise in the paddocks. But remember this: 'There's no such thing as an each-way bet in politics.'

Frankie had woken up at 7 a.m. on Sunday and it was then that 'it hit me what I had done. I just thought, "Mama mia!"' He attended Newmarket's Catholic Church 'to thank the Lord for the fantastic day I had on Saturday'. Then it was off to Ascot – again without his fiancée Catherine, who had the flu – for another day's racing!

By this time the journalists were desperate to locate our big winner for the Monday story. I knew now that William Hill were going to face a total loss of some £8 million – pretty disastrous, but not completely catastrophic; we would still be able to trade as usual, albeit with anticipated annual profits rather lower. I also knew that, though our mega-winner had actually won a total of £550,823.54, in normal circumstances he would only receive our upper-limit payout of £500,000. All bookmakers have to impose limits to cover them for just this type of situation. Unlike lottery or pools operators who can only ever pay out a proportion of what they take in – and therefore can never lose – bookmakers are obliged to pay everyone who bets on a winning result or a combination of such results, in full up to their limit, and could theoretically, therefore, go bust, which would do no one a great deal of good. And I knew that most winners who land a jackpot for even a modest amount like to keep quiet about it, for fear of envy – or worse – from neighbours, relatives and friends.

Having managed to get a phone number for Darren Yates, I rang him and found him undeniably euphoric, yet minded to retreat behind closed doors. He knew he had exceeded our limit, but was impressed when I told him by how much. So I made him an offer he didn't refuse: go public and I'll give you another fifty grand! In other words, we would offer him the total return from his bet. As a further inducement, my colleague David Hood had already ascertained that Frankie himself would be willing to hand Darren his cheque.

Darren needed that extra cash. Because of problems getting paid by customers for whom he had done work, the six staff he employed were on the verge of losing their jobs. He had just been refused a reported £700 building society loan and was facing up to having to lay the workers off. He also told me about his wife's attitude to him backing Frankie, and I knew this would be a key element in the media story – as would Darren's Dad, Charlie, who, it transpired, had also won £10,000 on Frankie's horses that day. (Charlie, though, remained a tad disappointed that he had not been trusting enough to follow Darren's advice to back all seven of Frankie's mounts, and had left two of them off his betting slip.) Darren's mum, Jacqueline, later described her son 'in tears when he rushed round to us telling us he had won. All he kept saying was how he was going to repay us for everything we had done for him.' I also concluded from our phone conversation that Darren Yates was something of an optimist – he'd placed the same bet on Frankie's Sunday rides!

Sometimes you have to work hard to sell a story to the press. Not this time. The moment I revealed that our big winner was prepared to enter the public domain, I was knocked over in the rush. The story took off with a life of its own. It landed the next day on the front pages of the *Daily Mail* and *Express*, and the *Guardian* told readers that Darren 'earned £300 on a good week. It takes a very long time,' it commented of his win, 'to earn that sort of money knocking in nails.' By the time people were opening their morning newspapers, Darren and family had been whisked down to London to be introduced to the nation on *GMTV* and interviewed by Anthea Turner – with the very pleasant surprise of Frankie Dettori himself turning up to congratulate them. 'He is my hero!' enthused the new half-millionaire. 'I could have kissed the ground he was galloping on!'

AT ASCOT THAT SUNDAY, Frankie was photographed with William Hill's Mike Burton and Ladbroke's Mike Dillon shaking him warmly by the throat. 'Don't expect for me to do it again today,' he warned a windswept Sue Barker, who was presenting *Sunday Grandstand* for the BBC. Television viewers were treated to a reprise of all seven races, followed by a tribute to Frankie from the suave Sir Peter O'Sullevan that placed him in the glorious tradition of Lester Piggott, Scobie Breasley and Gordon Richards. Then betting correspondent Graham Rock reported from the ring, 'scene of the Battle of Ascot 1996, when the punters routed the bookies'. Rock interviewed a doleful Mike Burton and a rueful Gary Wiltshire, who was wearing a black tie, but still convinced that he'd had no option but to take on the punters: 'The price of the last one was ridiculous – if you can't lay that, you shouldn't be a bookie. It was the best gamble of my life!'

'What if he does it again?' inquired Rock.

'I'll be in that river over there,' insisted Wiltshire.

Up north a defiant Fred Done was calling the punters back in for more – keeping his generous multiple-bet bonuses in place, and flashing a message up on all of his betting-shop screens: REWARD, DEAD OR ALIVE: GOOD-LOOKING ITALIAN KID, LAST SEEN IN ASCOT AREA.

John Hanmer, at home today, took a call from jockey Cash Asmussen, whom he acted for in Britain. Asmussen, riding in France, wanted to know who'd won at Ascot on Saturday. 'Dettori,' Hanmer told him. 'Who won the other races?' said Asmussen. 'It took me ten minutes to convince Cash that Frankie had won the lot,' says Hanmer.

The nightmare for the bookies ended with the first race of the day, when Sunbeam Dance, Frankie's 7/2 mount, faded to finish fourth. He ended the day with only one win out of his seven rides – Altamura in the last. Staking £1 on each of his seven mounts would have produced a payout of £7.50! Gary Wiltshire, though, had gone home after three races. 'People had read the papers and no one would bet with me,' he said. 'They thought I wouldn't be able to pay out.' I faced up to the media in a happier frame of mind than twenty-four hours earlier and told them, 'If he had repeated his success today there would have been a line of bookmakers queuing to jump off the stands.' 'The bookmakers were able to return the revolvers and bottles of whisky to the drawers after the champion jockey failed to emulate his historic feat,' reported *The Times*.

OVER AT LADBROKES MY counterparts had a problem or two with their own big winner. Mary Bolton had not just exceeded their limit – also of £500,000: she had almost doubled it, with her winnings on paper actually adding up to more than £900,000. They must have wondered if, once their mega-winner was unmasked, they would be criticized for holding back almost half of her payout. Mary Bolton was reluctant to agree to publicity, but eventually agreed to be named and to a public presentation of her cheque from Frankie – but Ladbrokes would not give her more than the half a million. They also had to pay 'several winners of over £100,000'.

Mary was far more gracious than I may have been in similar circumstances. 'It's a really nice amount without being greedy,' she told me when I spoke to her four years on – although her three children, Edward, Zoe and James, apparently demanded their pound of flesh with early Christmas present bids. 'Ladbrokes arranged for us to meet Henry Cecil,' she added, 'in fact, we refused to attend a cheque presentation unless they did – and he was charming.' A Ladbrokes insider, meanwhile, told me blithely that Mary was 'a bit like that woman who won the million on Chris Tarrant's *Who Wants To Be A Millionaire* – she didn't really need the extra money.' That's OK, then – she obviously won't miss four hundred grand.

Nor did the Boltons forget the source of their windfall – sending Frankie a solid silver calendar in recognition of his feat, which they were touched to see him drawing attention to in *Horsing Around*, a video featuring his career highlights. Frankie called it his 'favourite memento' of that day, and showed the inscription: 'Frankie: Thanks For A Day In A Million – The Boltons'. Husband John, whose own calculations had put their winnings at a mere £300,000, had waited for an hour at Ascot to thank Frankie personally. Mary was back at work on Monday morning – 'I couldn't let them down, could I?'

It could be construed as a little churlish to blame Ladbrokes for sticking to their limit, except that I have spent the last quarter of a century being churlish to Ladbrokes whenever possible. After all, on 1 October 1996 the *Financial Times* reported that

> . . . up to a third of the bookmaking industry's £100 million annual profits were wiped out by jockey Frankie Dettori's unprecedented seven horse triumph at Ascot. Stanley Leisure, the fourth biggest bookmaker yesterday issued a profits warning after losing £2.25 million on Saturday's race meeting. William Hill and Ladbrokes, the two biggest bookmakers, are understood to have lost about £8 million each, while Coral, third biggest, lost an estimated £4 million. Bookmakers would normally regard a payout of £2 million as a bad result on a Grand National.

Tom Kelly of BOLA was quoted on the industry's losses: 'It could be £30m, but could be higher still.' Paddy Bolger, Finance Director of Surrey Group, estimating a £100,000 loss, told the *FT*, 'This was a catastrophe for the betting industry.' On that Monday, Stanley Leisure shares fell by 8½ pence to £2.33½, while Bass, owners of Coral, suffered a 5½ pence fall; and Ladbrokes' weakened by an initial 3 pence, later rallying – possibly when they decided not to hand over that extra £400,000. The *FT* estimate of 'up to a third' may have erred on the side of caution – William Hill's Annual Report would comment that 'margins were generally satisfactory but were adversly affected' by Frankie – and their annual profit was £8,258,000 – about the amount they lost on that day.

ALL THE BIG BOOKMAKERS were licking their wounds. Fred Done, who has become infamous in recent seasons for paying out early to punters who back his favourite, Manchester United, to win the Premiership title, still recalls that Saturday afternoon as 'the worst day of my life. I sat down and filled out a full chequebook that day. The smallest one I wrote was for £25,000. It cost me £1.5 million.'

Mind you, there was an element of self-destruction in Done's losses. It had been Fred's decision to offer punters in all his 180 shops bonuses on multiple bets of up to 500 per cent for wagers involving six selections. Their biggest payout was £202,000 to a man from Newton le Willows. He turned out, ironically enough, to be an Italian ice cream seller who used his winnings to finance winter trips home. 'And there was a dear seventy-year-old lady from Salford who nearly collapsed when she found out she'd won £57,000 for under £1.' Fred finally went home, mentally exhausted, only to discover the day had one more unpleasant shock in store. His own gardener had won £10,000 on Frankie's horses – on a bet written on a William Hill betting slip, but placed with Fred Done!

Irish bookies Paddy Power reported that one man won £132,000 at a Dublin branch.

Tote Credit's biggest loss was to Mark Mallin, an investment banker from New York who won £250,000 with a 50p each way Super Heinz: 'I liked three or four of his rides,' he remembers, 'and figured I'd give it a go. I kept phoning Tote Credit to see how much I might win, because I wanted to hedge.'

Decorator John Squibb, thirty-nine, had backed Frankie's winners with Chris Prescott, a bookie based in Hornchurch in Essex, because 'I saw him on *A Question of Sport* and liked his face.' Prescott wasn't keen on the punter's face when he walked out of his shop £25,000 richer. It was Prescott's birthday, too!

Lancashire man Mick Reilly, fifty-two, backed Frankie, 'because my wife fancies him', and turned £1.80 into £1,452 – after which I dare say they both fancied Frankie.

Andrew Wilson from Stockton on Tees won £15,528 from 35 × 5p trebles and a 10p accumulator.

Martin Chiswell of Stourbridge, West Midlands was £12,880 better off; Michael Jaksic from Brighton, who had won £14,000 three weeks earlier, landed a £59,000 coup this time. Michael Squance of Southend banked £25,000. In Coventry engineering worker Ashok Gill bet £13.08 and collected £60,000. I even received an e-mail from an internet site correspondent reporting that 'A friend of mine bought a pub with the proceeds from his winnings that day.'

To give you more of an idea of the sheer scale of the monetary mayhem, I can do little better than reprise a press release I wrote and distributed on the Monday following the meeting.

Cornish Winner Is Pasty-Faced
After £200,000 Dettori Win

A William Hill punter who has £203,000 to collect from a Frankie Dettori bet has not visited the Truro, Cornwall branch where she placed her £9.81 wager on Saturday afternoon. 'A lady placed the bet at 10.15 on Saturday morning, laying out 35 twenty pence doubles and a one pound each-way accumulator on Dettori's seven mounts – but she has not been in to collect her winnings – surely she can't be unaware that they all won?' said William Hill spokesman Graham Sharpe.

William Hill's 1600 betting shops were paying out over £8 million to successful Dettori punters, including Darren Yates of Morecambe who won £550,000 and Leeds' punter George Michnik who collected £87,814.

Hills also paid out £357,600 to a Caernarfon customer; £166,000 to an Edinburgh client (staff later regretted telling this punter that his stake had been insufficient to cover his bet, as he had duly stumped up the extra amount, increasing his winnings by about £100,000); £193,222 to a Nottingham punter and £331,000 to a London gambler.

'We have seen bigger queues at the payout windows of our shops than for Lester Piggott winning the Derby; Red Rum winning the National or Desert Orchid winning the Gold Cup' said Hill's Graham Sharpe. 'And, Frankly, we DO give a damn!'

The Truro bet was collected on Tuesday and turned out to belong to a husband and wife couple who opted for no publicity.

On the Tuesday afterwards, Frankie was at Newmarket to make an official presentation: cheques to a total value of £1,036,322.46 to Darren Yates, £250,000 to Mark Mallin – who caused something of a stir by insisting the Tote had underpaid him by £10,000 – and £235,508.92 to Coral winner Steve Bolton, who had staked just £4.17. At Frankie's behest, each bookie donated £500 to three racing charities: the Injured Jockeys' Fund, the Stable Lads' Welfare Trust and the Fortune Riding Centre.

WILLIAM HILL'S OPERATIONS MANAGER, Liam McGuigan, had heard the news on Saturday while out shopping, and started planning immediately. He met with his regional directors and financial executives at 9 a.m. on Sunday before their 1,500-plus betting shops opened for business, to ensure they would be able to pay out to every winning customer by Monday morning. They had to contact banks throughout England, Scotland and Wales, provide shops with enough chequebooks, and revise their 'permission to pay' regulations to speed up payouts to five-figure winners.

In Scotland, William Hill's shop managers had scheduled their annual golf outing for the Sunday. 'As we arrived at the course on the bus,' says Alan McEwen, the manager of the Broughty Ferry branch (and subsequently the *Racing Post* Betting Shop Manager of the Year in 1999), 'every manager had tales of big winners, either from their own branches, or bets that they had checked from others. Each of us had convinced ourselves that our jobs were at severe risk.' The last golfer to arrive was district manager Jim Ward, who told them that he and his fellow line managers were being called in to collate the liabilities, an emergency board meeting had been called and there was a real danger of the company folding. With the look of condemned men they approached the first tee . . .

At this point the previously unappreciated talent of Frankie Dettori as a golf coach came into play. 'As most amateur golfers will agree,' explains Alan, 'you can fill your head with all kinds of nonsense as you begin your swing. "Is my grip okay? Left arm straight? Feet too far apart?" On this occasion there were no such thoughts going through our heads and consequently, to a man, we all scored well. Golf lesson number one – tee off with plenty of worries.'

After the morning round and an enjoyable lunch, Jim the district manager had returned. Although there had indeed been some very big returns throughout the country, it now seemed things were not as bad as first thought, and there was no chance of the company collapsing. 'Afternoon scoring,' says Alan McEwen, 'was extremely poor.'

On the Sunday 90 per cent of Hill's branches were open to offer customers cheque payments that day or cash payments the next. Managers were asked to resettle all winning bets to facilitate an accurate calculation of the total payment. A message was placed on the betting shop screen system congratulating all winning punters. By 4 p.m. on Monday everyone who wanted paying out had been paid – by which time the full extent of the financial setback was known. Liam McGuigan says that Channel 4 Racing, and the *Morning Line* in particular, have raised the public profile of jockeys to the extent that they now attract more regular followers than ever, and 'for weeks after, every time Frankie rode a winner or two we began to get very nervous'.

AT THE SAME TIME, Coral were also shelling out: £260,000 to one happy punter, £250,000 to another, with many more payouts between £25,000 and £60,000. One of their big winners, Peter Saxton, who spent £32.70 on his Super Heinz, worked in a betting shop himself in Poynton, Cheshire, and confirmed that his boss was mightily relieved the £247,000 winnings were not coming out of his pocket.

In the Battersea branch, recalls its Deputy Manager, Kevin Nightingale, one punter landed a bet for over £41,000 after selecting the first five winners, and kindly left a tip for £20 between the four staff. 'I had to laugh when it transpired that he had been overpaid by £100.' Kevin himself had placed a multiple bet on Frankie – the day before. 'Suffice to say I believe somebody "up there" was trying to tell me something,' he reflects, 'and I now only bet on the Grand National.'

Coral's Jason Brautigam – now, ironically, the Marketing Manager at Ascot – had been a Dettori fan ever since his first Group Race success in the Queen Elizabeth II Stakes in 1990. 'In fact, a Frankie Yankee was a staple part of my betting diet every Saturday.' So Jason backed five of Frankie's horses and duly won £240. However, it was the last Saturday of Coral's financial year, 'and Frankie's success cost me my annual bonus, which would have worked out at £880!'

AT LADBROKES THE ENORMITY of Dettori's achievement was realized first thing Monday morning when, following the shop returns, a loss of nearly £10 million was estimated. 'Ladbrokes were always concerned about the impact of media coverage on its shareholders, so everything had to be toned down and underplayed,' says Simon Clare, then one of Ladbroke's three PR managers, who had already blotted his copybook by reacting to the news of the Magnificent Seven as 'an enthusiastic racing fan'.

Our boss at the time, John O'Reilly, marched into our office at about 10 a.m., and announced that our sole objective over the next few days was to get as much positive publicity for Ladbrokes to make a £10 million loss worthwhile – absolutely no pressure on us, then! It was like playing a part in a politically correct pantomime, where all the supposed baddies are good guys really, and everyone gets on really well. It seemed out of kilter with the public's view that the evil bookies had been bashed by the white knight, Dettori, and the least we could do was to play our part, and moan and groan and be miserable about it. Of course, I had the sense to speak very gravely and with great seriousness when discussing the matter with senior Ladbrokes' personnel, but in reality I thought it was exciting and loved the frenzied media attention that came with it.

We were quickly presented with a list of every bet that had cost Ladbrokes £1,000 or more – it was about a hundred pages thick, with ten names on each, and I wish I still had a copy of it, because it made heart-warming reading. Nearly every single winner was an ordinary betting-shop regular, who had placed a small stake multiple bet on all Dettori's rides. Even those who had won the bigger amounts had simply been the punters who had had the foresight to take prices on all seven horses. These were nearly all the so-called 'mug punters', blindly following the top jockey of the day, placing bets that most shrewd punters would never dream of placing – 20p Heinzes, 50p accumulators, £5 Yankees on the TV races – stereotypical betting-shop punters, from every town and county in England, and it was truly their day in the sun.

I found just one betting shop manager who refused to believe that Frankie had caused the business any problem at all. Patrick McIntyre, then working for A.R. Dennis in St Albans, told me that the previous Saturday Coastal Bluff had won the Gold Cup at Ayr, 'a result that everyone in the country knew was going to happen', and of the twelve shops he was co-ordinating, eleven phoned up requesting money for Monday to pay for the result. 'In contrast, only one of the twelve shops needed money after Frankie's Seven.' Here is Patrick's explanation:

If I remember, the QE II was considered a three-horse race, of which Mark of Esteem was the shortest price of the three. And William Hill's price, which we used in our shops, was the shortest on offer. This meant that the QEII was a brilliant result for the shops – Mark of Esteem was virtually unbacked. Diffident was also an exceptional result as it was not fancied at all. By the time the public caught on, the prices were too low to do any damage. Most multi-bets missed out Diffident and the other big-priced winner, and the shops had decent to good results. They also cleaned up when everyone backed Frankie's mounts on the Sunday and the following Saturday. It certainly wasn't the disaster the bookies tried to make it out to be. In fact, with the publicity on front and back pages it was probably the best day in the history of bookmaking.

Well, I am not entirely sure I could go along with that view, which makes the case for the Loch Ness Monster look convincing, but Patrick is entitled to it.

MOST PUNTERS WHO CASHED in on Frankie's day of a lifetime were able to collect their winnings without any problems, but with tens of thousands picking up hefty wedges it would be a minor miracle had there not been the slightest hiccup. Michael Singer, an indefatigable critic of bookmakers who was once instrumental in the now-defunct National Association for the Protection of Punters, could come up with just one.

Andrea Smith from South Shields was a devoted Dettori fan – the signed photograph he had sent her had pride of place in her family's front room. She had the same bet every Saturday: a £1 double, a £1 placepot and a 50p each-way accumulator. On the historic day, as usual, she wrote the double at the top of the bet. Both horses lost. But the accumulator horses were the first six winners of Frankie's seven, which meant she'd won some £4,300. 'When Frankie's sixth winner went in, my family were all running round like lunatics,' she told Claude Duval, the *Sun*'s 'Punter's Pal', who took up her case. 'My husband Jimmy was out of work and I thought that I could give my three children a really wonderful Christmas.' But when she went to collect from Simonside Bookmakers, the proprietor told her she'd had an eight-horse accumulator – and therefore refused to pay out.

'He was very rude to me and told me to "**** off". He claimed that I had an eight-horse accumulator and, as the first two had lost, he had nothing to pay me.'

Claude Duval took up her case:

With a photographer I visited Richard Jary's scruffy, tiny, back-street betting shop. It was deserted. His son Peter was behind the counter and claimed that his father was not present that day. Later we saw Jary's face peep behind the counter and it was duly photographed. The photographer and I were subjected to a barrage of abuse. I was quite relieved to board the Inter-City express back to London.

For many years I waged a war of words with the *Sporting Life's* Green Seal service. I was absolutely convinced that in the vast majority of betting disputes the Green Seal service found in favour of the bookies. You didn't have to be a member of Mensa to realize that the *Life* survived very largely on bookies' advertisements. Andrea took her case to the Green Seal service and, predictably, they found in favour of Jary. It was scandalous.

There was another avenue of appeal. Facing the Tattersall's Committee, a body of worthies set up in 1929 to settle betting disputes, was quite a daunting experience for Andrea Smith. The *Sun* paid the non-returnable deposit. Jary sat in as Andrea gave her evidence. I reported my visit to the shop and the fact that I had taken up the case because I passionately believed that what had happened was a terrible injustice.

The verdict of Tattersalls was that Andrea should receive half her winnings – £2,150. Jary stormed off saying, 'I'll sue you.' But he later paid up. I still believe she should have received the full amount. Either she had the bet, or she didn't. The result was something of a fudge.

Andrea blew quite a lot of the cheque for £2,200 on a massive party at which they drank 'a fantastic Frankie punch. I've never been back to that betting shop,' she adds, 'and I told all my friends to boy-cott the place.'

NOW LET'S HEAR ABOUT several people who didn't win fortunes on Frankie's Magnificent Seven – though they should have done. Paul Lawrence from Ealing, known to his friends as 'China', is a regular racegoer who always bets on Frankie – and particularly at Ascot, whose Royal meeting in June often coincides with his birthday. Having enjoyed the 1996 Royal meeting so much, he booked another lunch table at the Festival for eight of his friends, including Eddie Gorniak, who tells what happened: 'Paul *always* has a Lucky 126 bet on Frankie to a £1 unit, hardly ever making a profit. But China would never give up on his hero, saying things like, "Frankie's a good thing in this one, he always wins when he wears green." It had become a running joke, so when we turned up in September on the minibus, having had a few beers, the ribbing started: "Are you doing the Frankie yankee, China?" So much so that China was eventually shamed into not putting on his normal bet.'

Then Frankie Dettori went through the card.

'We couldn't believe it,' says Eddie. 'I think we all felt a bit guilty – and to this day I've never dared work out what it would have come to.' All China won that day was £279 on the Tote's Jackpot.

Also in their party, however, were John and Debbie West – John, someone who enjoyed a serious bet, Debbie, a £2 each-way punter. 'Every time we went to Ascot they'd have the same argument,' says Eddie. 'He wanted to put lots on and she would tell him to be sensi-ble. Anyway, this was the day when the roles were reversed. I'd fancied Mark of Esteem but changed my mind after Frankie won the first two races. But Debbie backed him anyway. She had suddenly changed and announced, "I'm going to put all my winnings on Frankie again." This was where John woke up – "Put some on and save some." She ignored him and won again. She put the lot on the next one – and continued doing so right up to and including the last race. It was really funny seeing the serious gambler John trying to stop her putting it all on the last – but she did, and cleaned up.

'As for China,' says Eddie, 'he even lost money in the pub that night playing heads or tails with pound coins stacked up. If this gets printed and you are reading it, sorry, mate!'

Pete Gwilliam, whom we met earlier on in his hospitality box at the course, was the 'alleged racing expert of the party', as he puts it, 'so the responsibility for making selections often ended up with me. I am ashamed to say I found five horses to be second to Frankie, but, most painfully, chose to lay all the party's bets on Fujiyama Crest at starting price plus one point, since I thought it was eight to ten points shorter than its form deserved. The roar of the crowd and the emotion of being part of history – albeit a losing part of history – meant that seeing Fujiyama bravely respond to Frankie's urgings was a special moment rather than a suicidal one. So I can safely claim to have had the worst day's betting – and laying – of my life, but the best day's racing.'

PAT EPTON, THE LINCOLNSHIRE cleaner who had had 50 pence on each of Frankie's winners, collected her winnings of £19. Had she invested the additional 50p for an accumulator covering all seven, she would have netted an additional £12,047.50 – at Starting Price odds, anyway. Taking the Early Bird prices would have produced about £120,000. She was philosophical about the outcome – to me, unconvincingly so: 'What you haven't got, you don't miss.'

CHAPTER ELEVEN

'SHOULD YOUR BOOK EVER BE MADE INTO A FILM, THE SOUNDTRACK
TO THE LAST RACE SHOULD BE "WITH A LITTLE HELP FROM MY
FRIENDS"'

ANONYMOUS TELEPHONE CALLER TO THE AUTHOR

THE MAGNIFICENT SEVEN MAY have made sporting history, but that history was not made without controversy. Two
issues attracted prolonged, often acrimonious debate. Firstly,
and almost instantly, the returned Starting Price of Fujiyama
Crest; and secondly, but not in any meaningful public way until
much later, whether the final race had been truly competitive.

To pursue this latter line of inquiry is to court considerable criticism
and displeasure. No less a man than Channel 4 racing pundit John
McCririck registered great disapproval of my even raising the issue,
feeling that to do so might somehow demean Frankie's achievement. Sir
Peter O'Sullevan was also reluctant to discuss the matter, remarking
simply that 'all the jockeys would be riding for their lives, there's no
doubt about that'. But I disagree with them – it seems to me it would be
negligent not at least to address the considerable groundswell of rumour
and suspicion that lingered after the immediate euphoria had died down.

I posted a request for memories of the day on a racing website,
theracingforum.co.uk. Amongst those who responded was T.F.J.
Gould, who wrote:

> I think Frankie was 'helped' in the last race by being given a virtually
> uncontested lead. I remember backing a John Dunlop horse who
> patently needed to lead and was somewhat surprisingly held up by
> Jason Weaver, normally a good judge of pace. The same horse came
> out next time and won, making all in a similarly competitive handicap
> over c & d [course and distance]. My overall impression at the time
> was that Eddery was the only one giving 100%.

Weaver finished fifteenth on Flocheck, 'always behind', according to *Raceform*, a horse 'suited by forcing tactics' in the respected opinion of *Racehorses of 1996*. Flocheck – who had made the running when second under Pat Eddery at Yarmouth over 2¼ miles last time out – did, indeed, win next time out ('chased leaders, led 9f out, made rest', said Superform). This was at odds of 9/1, at Ascot, over the same extended 2 mile trip on 11 October, albeit on good to soft going – compared to this day's firm side of good ground, and partnered by Mick Kinane. Pat Eddery, on 5/2 favourite Northern Fleet – runner-up to Fujiyama Crest – finished back in fifth place. Flocheck carried 3lbs more than Northern Fleet this time, having been burdened with 8lbs more than his rival in the previous race. A correspondent styling himself 'Insider' wrote: 'As for Fujiyama Crest, it must be said, he was not exactly challenged very forcefully.'

Writer Jamie Reid has been around the racetrack, the ring and the betting scene for many years. Currently writing a weekly tipping column for the *Guardian*, he has always preferred to take the punters' side against the bookies. Had he heard any hints that the last race wasn't the most competitive event ever run?

> Definitely. Absolutely. There was a massive feeling about that, amongst the professionals and regulars, not only those silly racegoers talking through their pockets – the regulars who bet seriously seemed to feel that somehow or other he would do it in the last. In fact it got us thinking back to other legendary occasions, like the time a member of the Aussie cricket team touring here in the early '60s, found himself in big financial trouble, having opened up a betting account with a famous bookie not a million miles removed from William Hill, which he couldn't pay. The story was that a few of the Aussie jockeys on the circuit 'helped out' in the last race on the card one day – and the player duly won all his money back from other bookmakers, and settled up with the one to whom he was in debt!

Perhaps most outspoken on the last race was well known tipster Mark Winstanley, in the subscription-only *Sports Adviser* magazine. He was reacting to an article by *Racing Post* archivist and statistician John Randall – now famous for winning £500,000 on *Who Wants To Be A Millionaire* – who had written a feature declaring Frankie's ride on Fujiyama Crest the tenth greatest of the last 100 years. 'I must take issue,' declared Winstanley. 'Apart from Pat Eddery on the runner-up, it seemed to me that the rest of the jockeys were happy to let Frankie get to the front from stall one – not an easy task on the two-mile course at Ascot. Having watched the video many times I'm left believing that the result may have been different if that race had been the first and not the last on the card.' 'I think it just turned out to be a jockeys' race,' argues Warwick Bartlett, the BBOA Chairman. 'Whether intentional or not, psychologically everyone else seemed de-energized. This doesn't mean to say that anything happened which was untoward.' He also believes that, 'In the last race, only Pat Eddery seemed to be really trying to beat Fujiyama Crest.' Warwick told me, 'Had it been the first race, there is no doubt in my mind that he [Frankie] would not have won.'

Ben Newton, acting editor of the *Sporting Life* that day, felt obliged to check out such uncertainties, 'asking one or two professional punters whether they had heard that anyone in the race had, shall we say, not been at their busiest – but as time went on we decided it was not an avenue we should go down'. Tom Clarke, the editor of the *Sporting Life*, recalled 'lots of talk of that nature – after the euphoria died down, many wondered whether the last race had been totally competitive'. John Hanmer, who knew Fujiyama Crest well and regarded him as a 'pretty unwilling' type, heard a friend who had backed Northern Fleet and Pat Eddery complain, 'I bet he didn't try.' But John himself is nevertheless adamant: 'Pat just hated getting beaten and he gave it everything in the last.' It should not be forgotten that Pat was at the time the sole holder of the record for the number of winners on one day – seven, albeit in an afternoon/evening double stint. Eddery himself told *Racing Post* (16 May 2001), 'I am out there to win. Whatever sort of race it is, I want to win. That is how it has always been for me, ever since day one.'

I came across more than one suggestion that the outcome was

actually preordained. There is absolutely no evidence, or even hint, that Frankie himself could have had a hand in any moves to ensure he won the last – unthinkable. Nor is a quickly convened get-together of the other jockeys agreeing amongst themselves to give Frankie the run of the race remotely plausible. But a winner does not need to know, and may not even suspect, that he is being allowed or assisted to win. In one infamous snooker game involving Jimmy White there was convincing evidence that his opponent had been playing to lose – yet White was exonerated of all blame. He did not know what was happening. Certainly Frankie would later say of the seventh race that, with just 4 furlongs to run, he was 'surprised nobody came and took me on'.

According to a hugely knowledgeable observer of the on-course racing scene, one of the jockeys in the last race had told him that, Frankie being a popular rider who had made few enemies, most of those riding in the last had decided they would have no problem if he managed to win it. (My source did exclude Pat Eddery from this suggestion on the grounds of his 'professional jealousy'.)

A similar tale was imparted to off-course bookmaker John Nelson. 'No outsider could ever know whether anything untoward went on,' he says, 'but everybody in the dressing room was anticipating something big which would benefit the racing industry – they were all patting him on the back. Someone close to the action said to me I shouldn't be wasting time asking about betting patterns but looking at the running of the race.'

In January 2001 Derek McGovern, weekly tipster for the *Mirror* and a man not afraid to speak his mind, treated readers of the Zoobet website to an article entitled 'Is It Fixed?'

Am I the only one who thinks racing provides too many heartwarming results to be explained by mere coincidence? I have watched over the last decade or so a string of races in which it was easy to suspect more than Fate played a part. Dettori's seventh winner of the afternoon at Ascot; Peter Scudamore's last-ever ride, also at Ascot; Declan Murphy's tear-jerking comeback at Chesptow; the similarly brave return from injury of Walter Swinburn at Haydock; more recently the turf farewells of Reg Akehurst and Peter O'Sullevan. All produced winners for the characters centre stage.

McGovern went on to point out that both Frankie Dettori himself and Ray Cochrane had won on their return to action after their plane crash.

I know of one representative of a leading bookmakers who believes his firm should stop betting on such races because the outcome is almost inevitable; and of punters who triple their stakes when such opportunities arise . . .

I am not saying that the above races were bent: for goodness sake, I want no part of a month-long libel trial. What I am suggesting is that there are surely grounds for suspicion . . . Is there not the teensiest chance in all of this that other jockeys allowed these horses to win, not for sinister reasons, but as an acknowledgement of the services to their sport of the likes of Scudamore, O'Sullevan, Dettori and Murphy? Almost certainly they did not pre-arrange the outcome but perhaps decided not to try 100 per cent once it became clear a more heartwarming result was on the cards.

Of course all this speculation could be utter nonsense. There is an equally strong chance that these horses won purely because their jockeys, owners or trainers recognised their importance as milestones and prepared them with a diligence unsustainable over the course of a whole season.

McGovern concludes, however, that, even if the conspiracy theorists were proved right, this would effectively be a victimless crime. 'The over-riding point about all this is that, even if punters suspect stage-management, we are not unduly worried. In many ways we can admire such esprit de corps.'

For a final word on this, I asked my William Hill colleague David Hood, who had a previous career as a jump jockey for top trainers like former champion jump jockey Stan Mellor. Modestly self-effacing about his own 'strictly inauspicious career in the saddle', David nevertheless found any conspiracy theory that the last race was, despite the narrow margin of victory, somehow 'handed' to Frankie very difficult to accept.

The only thing I do believe is that there will have been such heightened awareness of the occasion that riding tactics may have been changed or exaggerated, consequently working in Frankie's favour. Several of the jockeys have since told me their orders were to 'watch Frankie – don't let him get away'. This allowed Dettori to bounce along in front, poaching a lead that in normal circumstances would not have been afforded to him.

But from the bottom of your boots you want to ride winners – especially on big race days. There can be no doubt that they would have all been wishing him the best of luck as they went out to ride, and there would have been a lot of back-slapping going on. But the competitive spirit that drives everybody who has ever held a jockey's licence would have motivated so many of the lads to want to beat Frankie.

I was determined to discover Dettori's opinion of these contentious issues, and spoke to him in July 2001. He seemed slightly taken aback, as though he had never previously been asked to confront the thought, when I asked how he would have approached the race had it been first on the card. After pondering a little, he confessed that he 'might have been a little more cautious and got beat', whereas given the prevailing situation, 'I was bold. I told myself, "I'm not going to let this bastard spoil it for me." I didn't care at all, **** it, off we go.' I asked him how he would have approached the race if Pat, Ray or Jason had been on a seven-timer – 'I don't think I'd have ridden any differently.' I then enquired as to whether anyone ever suggested to him that any of the other jockeys took it easy? 'You should have seen Pat's face after the race – he was not very pleased at all. His horse had looked the one to beat. He wasn't happy.'

Four days after the event, Warwick Bartlett, Chairman of the British Betting Offices Association, representing the smaller to medium-sized betting shop group owners, addressed the question of Fujiyama Crest's starting price, in a belligerent letter to the *Sporting Life*:

> We need to scrutinise the system where bookmakers send money back to the course. Frankly, the system failed on Saturday and, as the weeks unfold, the true cost of supporting an out-of-date racecourse betting operation will become apparent. There has been much talk that Fujiyama Crest was realistically a 10/1 chance because that was his price in the morning. The price in the morning was based on the opinion of the twenty or so people who provide the 'tissue' for the off-course market. They were wrong; the horse won like a good thing.
>
> What was also wrong was the horse's starting price which should reflect the money staked. The betting shows on Racing Data were: 5/2, 2/1, 7/4, 2/1, 9/4, 2/1 SP. Can someone tell me how a horse that is a loser in the industry's field book for £10 million can shorten to 7/4 then drift to 9/4? William Hill, the Tote, Ladbrokes all piled in at 7/4; the result was that the next show was 2/1. It should have been evens. Indeed, were a Tote system in operation, the horse would have been 1/4.
>
> When Fujiyama Crest hit 2/1, that was when the system crashed. It was at that point that phones were left unanswered in the trade rooms; it was at that point that bookmakers began to phone bookmakers they had not bet with for ten years to get on. No one would lay the 2/1 off-course and suddenly everyone's worst nightmare became a reality; the next show was 9/4. Nothing could be done at 9/4; the shutters were down.
>
> The race was off, the atmosphere electrifying in the offices. Then the result – the SP, 2/1. There is a god after all, the quarter point saving the industry £3 million.
>
> The system failed. Fujiyama Crest was returned 2/1 against, it should have been 1/4. Rails bookmakers who make a living not by making a book, take an opinion on a race and lay one horse. The 9/4 about a 10/1 chance seemed like manna from heaven. Dettori made it hell and we have to rely on their poor judgement for an SP.

Bartlett's letter was not allowed to pass unchallenged. Doug

Newton, the *Sporting Life*'s chief SP reporter, was outraged and leapt to the defence of the system:

> Some bookmakers really are their own worst enemies. Warwick Bartlett's letter says it all about the gulf between real, traditional bookmakers and the accountant-dominated betting shop operators. Regardless of the fact that his organisation professes to represent these rather than the big multiples, he objects to independents, who bet with their own money and don't have huge public companies' cash behind them, having any say in the course markets which produce the starting prices – as they have done so far with the apparent approval of off-course interests.
>
> No mention, also, of the untold times over the years since betting shops were legalised that SPs have been reduced to a 'realistic' rate by trade firms piling on the money at meetings up and down the country. He wants to scrap it all because a once-in-a-lifetime incident for once caught the bookies on the hop.
>
> He should know it was not just the rails bookmakers who were fielding against Fujiyama Crest – every layer worth his salt saw the value of laying 2/1 about a horse whose chance represented 12/1 according to the odds-making 'judges' on whom Bartlett and the rest of the industry are happy to rely the rest of the time. Many medium and small boards bookies got stuck in well above their normal limits and paid the penalty. And most of them were typically philosophical – indeed many said they would love to have the same value all the time regardless of which way results went.
>
> This thinking crystallises the difference between track bookies and most betting shop operators. Shop men expect a set profit from their investments regardless of what happens on the racecourse. They don't seem to see that when backed horses win, they lose, and vice versa; they just want a guaranteed return on their investment.

Hot on Newton's heels was Norman Miller, Chairman of the National Association of Bookmakers:

> Warwick Bartlett's conclusion that the SP system failed is extraordinary. A horse which was widely quoted at 10/1 and above in the

morning prices was returned 2/1 favourite. Over £300,000 in large bets was recorded by the SP returners. So what went wrong? He says betting shop bookmakers could not get on! But with whom? There are many on-course bookmakers offering reliable on-course hedging services to off-course bookmakers. They were not over-used at Ascot on Saturday. If the industry lost £30 million on Dettori's triumph, it follows that £10 million was riding on Fujiyama Crest. Surely more than £300,000 should have been sent back to the course.

No, Mr Bartlett, the system did not fail; the SP bookmakers were not in a position to protect themselves.

In the face of this barrage of criticism Bartlett, though, remained unrepentant: 'The NAB made a serious political error by not holding an enquiry. This day was a watershed, it changed how we viewed the ring. It highlighted its shortcomings, and brought to the authorities' attention that changes were necessary. The results [that outsiders have since been permitted to buy into racecourse betting pitches] have been costly to the industry, as amateurs who think they know better have meddled in affairs where they have no experience.'

Tom Kelly is Warwick's counterpart as Director General of the Betting Office Licensees Association, to which the major bookmaking chains belong. Confessing that his immediate reaction to the news of Dettori's seven-timer was, 'Oh, shit', he offered me his more considered view:

While the hedging system may work tolerably well in normal circumstances, it becomes near enough impotent when the racecourse bookmakers know that they are laying a horse at odds far shorter than those which would reflect its chance of winning. The outstanding example of this was the last race, in which the weight of money should have made Fujiyama Crest an odds-on chance, even if the form book said he should have been 10/1 or more.

Over the following days, some people said that the amount of publicity created by Frankie's 7-timer was compensation for the financial loss. This was not a view I heard endorsed by any bookmaker.

Never slow to miss a chance to kick out at betting shop operators, well-known *Racing Post* writer and punter Harry Findlay labelled Bartlett 'Hindsight Harry'. 'Funny,' he wrote, 'how we never hear him complain when Ladbrokes smash a horse from 4/1 to 7/4 on a wet and miserable Monday afternoon at Folkestone or Brighton with the amount of money I'd expect to spend on a half-decent bottle of wine!' But he did concede that

> . . . every independent bookmaker at Ascot on Saturday with either brains, balls or both had their biggest ever nightmare. Professional layers were getting the chance to lay a horse at 2/1 when not a serious punter in the country took the double-figure price freely available before Frankie's roll-up commenced. The layers who stuck [*sic*] into Fujiyama Crest had the bet of a lifetime. But it all went badly wrong. For the record, more bookmakers have complained to me about Mr Bartlett's letter than they have about Fujiyama Crest winning the race.

Warwick wasn't going to take that lying down.

> Let's turn the clock back to 1976. As John McCririck is my witness, I tried to introduce change on the rails. I displayed a TV and was told to remove it. I was the first bookmaker in that year to use a radio tele-phone. I was told to remove it. Even today only a few fixed telephone lines are allowed, mainly to the Big Three bookmakers [Hill, Coral, Ladbrokes]. Cellular phones can be used but they are unreliable in remote locations. So, after 20 years, little has been done to improve the flow of business to the course. If racecourse bookmakers lost money on Dettori it was their choice. They decided to lay the horse. We did not have the option and were denied the facility to hedge as the market closed down.

More heavy artillery was aimed in Bartlett's direction by veteran observer of the racing scene, Monty Court. 'In the days when Frankie Dettori was wearing nappies and riding nothing faster than a tricycle,' he blasted, 'my forthright old friend Richard Baerlein [racing writer for the *Guardian* and the *Observer*] declared: "The number one rule of all bookmakers is, *Thou shalt not win.*'" He continued:

Last Saturday, when the brilliant young Italian rode all seven Ascot winners and gave the nation's bookmakers a £30 million beating, it was the cue for Baerlein's words to come echoing down the years. It was the unbelievable day when all the unlikely and impossible bets that provide a non-stop torrent of money into betting shop coffers came good. After years of losing it was the mug-punters' revenge.

There had never been a day like it and, although most thinking men in the betting industry accepted the hammering philosophically, it wasn't long before we started to hear the squeals – not, it must be said, from those in the front-line on the racecourse, who tried to smile through their tears. In an outburst that suggested he might feel more at home leading a group of grocers, Warwick Bartlett blamed the system of betting shops sending money back to the course to shrink the odds, to suit off-course bookmakers and exclaimed: 'Saturday was when the chickens came home to roost'.

Wrong, Mr Bartlett, Saturday was when the chickens started to squawk.

Having had some while to think about the situation in the betting ring at Ascot on that day, the influential racing annual *Racehorses of 1996*, which emanated from the *Timeform* racehorse ratings stable, also adopted an unsympathetic tone towards off-course bookmakers. 'If ten million pounds was riding on Fujiyama Crest, why was only a reputed £300,000 or so sent back to the course. Did the starting price bookmakers in general, many of them accountant-dominated, really do enough to protect themselves?'

'After the fourth race it was a drop in the ocean,' responds Rob Hartnett, then of Coral. 'It was like trying to stem the tide. In the ring, bets were struck the likes of which had never been seen before. Bookmakers on their way out of business felt they had to lay 2/1 about a 12/1 chance, and in the heat of battle one could understand their logic. With hindsight, however, there really was no way out.'

But with an obvious delight at the discomfiture of the betting shop lobby and the irony of their criticisms, *Racehorses of 1996* observed slyly, 'Perhaps those among Mr Bartlett's members who claimed they were "denied the facility to hedge as the market closed down" now appreciate how their own customers feel sometimes when they can't get on!'

CHAPTER TWELVE

'YOU COULD ALMOST SEE THE BLOOD ON THE RAILS IN THE BETTING RING'

MIKE DILLON OF LADBROKES, WHO LOST A REPORTED £10 MILLION

PERHAPS THE BEST WAY to understand the psychology of both the on- and off-course sides of the betting industry that day is to hear the first-hand recollections of two of the major protagonists. First, here is the inside story of what went on in the epicentre of the giant William Hill operation, as told by Richard Banks, the acting Betting Control Director, who was responsible for Hill's liabilities.

Nothing unusual appeared to be happening, until Mark of Esteem won, when we trimmed the Early Bird odds of Fatefully from 9/2 to 7/2, and Fujiyama Crest from 11/1 to 8/1 – to cover the unlikely event of Frankie riding any further winners. We lost about £30,000 on the Mark of Esteem race. No build-up of money was to be seen at this point, however, I decided to back Decorated Hero to win £40,000, thinking that if this won at least we'd have that much to play up on Fatefully – although this was, at that stage, something of a tongue in cheek thought.

We lost nearly £70,000 on the Decorated Hero race. I knew now we were in trouble. My first thought was to try to prevent any further business being taken on his remaining mounts. The best way to do this was to shorten the Early Bird odds again. We went 5/2 from 7/2 about Fatefully, and 5/1 from 8/1 Fujiyama Crest. This made us the shortest prices available across the main bookmakers.

As 4.30 p.m. approached, our known liability, should Fatefully win, was approaching a third of a million pounds. So, true to my earlier tongue in cheek thought, we invested our £40,000, and with the help of Ladbrokes and Coral we managed to send Fatefully off at 7/4. Unfortunately it didn't stop it from winning. We further reduced the early bird odds for Fujiyama Crest to 3/1 from 5/1, but now if any trade clients wanted to take a price, we had unavoidably to inform them that we were accepting starting price odds only, as by now our liabilities were spiralling upwards. The Credit Race Room was buzzing and the LBO [Licensed Betting Office] Race Room was struggling to keep the 'running-up' money up to date. I needed to know the potential damage as soon as possible.

'Phone call for you.'

It was John Brown, the MD. I thought to myself, 'that's all I need right now!' John, I was surprised to hear, was actually at Ascot. He had been observing our on-course team and was satisfied with their performance so far under the prevailing circumstances. He asked what I intended to do with Lochangel. The liability was still growing and it looked as though we would lose nearly three-quarters of a million on the race. I told John the on-course staff were already putting £40,000 on as soon as anyone put up a price for Lochangel. John said he'd leave me to get on with it, but before I could get back to the job I took another call, this time from Dave Lowery [Group Racing Director]. I had a virtually identical conversation with him. Lochangel's price was 5/4. News was filtering back that Coral had hedged £80,000 and Ladbrokes £40,000, along with £45,000 from us – but the odds would not shorten any further. The majority of the on-course bookmakers were losing so much money already that they needed to take any money which came their way in an attempt to recoup their losses. They, too, believed that no jockey could ride six consecutive winners at Ascot.

Lochangel's race was over in what seemed like a flash – an amazing six-timer had been achieved. In a last ditch effort to avoid further support, we shortened Fujiyama Crest to a ridiculous price of 2/1 from 3/1. But punters and trade still kept coming for the horse. Some, I believe, just wanted to be part of potentially the most astounding sequence of races and rides ever to be witnessed. The Betting Control

Department was at 'all systems go' level. Running-on money was being checked in the Credit Race Room, and the LBO Race Room was struggling to check and input the figures individually. I instructed them to enter collective totals, in the hope that I would know the extent of the potential losses sooner. Other departmental heads called to find out whether we were coping. Further phone calls from Dave Lowery and John Brown, both asking 'How much did we have on the last one? How much are we winning through hedging? How much are we having on the next one?' I think, deep down, they both wished they were in the office with me to share the excitement, the tension, the pressure and the challenging decision-making.

The known liability for Fujiyama Crest stood at around £1.5 million. The majority of the running-on money was locked in at our original price of 11/1. We have always believed that the total win/loss figure is at least double what you can see in the known field book. Our on-course staff had invested £30,000 early to ensure a short early show. This was achieved, but then the odds got bigger. A reported £50,000 from Ladbrokes and £100,000 from Coral followed – but the odds just would not shorten below 2/1.

John Brown rang again and asked, 'How much have we had on?' I told him thirty-five. 'Is that all? Just keep putting it on.'

'We simply cannot shorten the odds,' I responded.

'I'll leave you to get on with it, then,' he said as he went into the betting ring to confirm what I was telling him. All the on-course bookmakers had 'done their bollocks', but 'knew' Dettori could not ride seven winners, and saw this last race as their salvation for the day. Our on-course rep informed me that Gary Wiltshire had pulled him to one side to ask him how much he wanted on at 2/1 as he had plenty to lay. We now believe that a number of off-course layers/entrepreneurs saw this as an ideal opportunity to lay a horse – albeit unofficially – with reasonably exposed form at 2/1, when the true betting odds against it winning were 11/1 or even greater – good business, if you can get it every day. I knew now there was no point in hedging more money as we would never affect the Starting Price.

As the off-time approached, Dave Lowrey rang to listen to a race commentary as relayed by me to him in his car with his wife, Hazel. My version of the race went something like 'they're turning into the straight. Fujiyama Crest is in the front rank and travelling well. There doesn't seem to be anything going too well.'

'We'll be all right,' Dave said reassuringly.

'I'm not so sure, he's still in front. We've only got one chance – go on Pat, go on Pat – hit it, hit it!' I shouted desperately, needing Eddery to get more animated (apologies to animal protection groups, but this was important) – 'NO, he's not going to get there – Dettori's done us!'

'Oh, dear' said Hazel, with classic understatement. Dave uttered something quite unprintable.

'£1.5 million in the fieldbook,' I said, anticipating his first question.

'Well, you can double that just for starters,' he groaned, and hung up.

The racing was over. The 25,095/1 seven-timer was achieved. The on-course bookmakers had been decimated by the off-course book-makers, but unfortunately we could not shorten the odds in the manner which we expected, which would have saved us hundreds of thousands. But at least they will think twice in future.

John Brown rang shortly afterwards to ask how much we had on the last race in total. I told him £35,000, to which he responded, 'I think you were right. You wouldn't have moved the price if you'd had twice as much on – anyway, well done.' That was by far the best phone call of the day.

I also invited on-course bookmaker Barry Dennis to look back on his actions that day. I am delighted he took the opportunity to produce such a remarkably honest assessment of what went on:

Frankie day. At the start I had been pleased because, for whatever reason, I had got the best move up I had ever had at a full Ascot meeting, about six in from the rails in the back row. A chance to play bigger than usual with the hoped-for bigger rollers.

Nothing unusual for the earlier races, holding about four grand a race, winning a bit, losing a bit, no great alarms. Come the fifth race a few punters commented that Frankie had ridden the first four winners. I just thought – so what, good achievement, but been done before. Didn't even bother to take note of his next mount, didn't notice any undue market moves in the fifth race. After the fifth there was now a buzz going round the ring – the offices must start to take action in the sixth race. I think they did invest, but not in any monster gamble.

Once the sixth race was over, all hell let loose – everyone was speculating what price the offices would take in the final race, the seventh. I understand that 6/1 was laid to small amounts on the outskirts of the ring. My eldest son, Patrick – at that stage he only worked for me on Saturdays and was a yuppie whizzkid in the city during the week – came rushing up to me and said, 'Coral are out in the ring taking 2/1 Fujiyama Crest' – and he could get 9/4 in the Silver Ring. I quickly put up 2/1 as well – I wanted to get as much as I could while they were still investing. It's not often – no, never – did I get a chance to mug the offices and lay such a price about a real 10/1 chance.

Shortly after, Hills and Ladbrokes were out doing the same thing. I thought at the time, what absolute cowards, why don't they stand up to the liabilities. It can't win, anyway, it's a bloody great handicap with plenty of horses who can, and will, beat it. Patrick came up to me and said could I lay a £2,000/£1,000 for him – at the time he was earning about £400 a week. His confidence brought new bravado to me and I called all the offices in and asked them how much they wanted. When they said 'you name it, all in', I laid them £11,000 at 2/1 – ten for me, one for Pat. Remember at that stage the most I had ever been forced to stand a horse for in my life had been £5,000.

The race is off. I do not feel any anxiety, everyone knows no jockey can ride all seven winners in such big races at an Ascot Festival. During the race I repeatedly switch from my bins to the big screen, but don't panic when he is leading from a long way out. I know, deep down, what he is trying to do is impossible. A furlong to go, still in front. Don't panic, something is coming to challenge him on the outside – this is going to beat him. I knew he couldn't ride all seven winners, it isn't possible. Half a furlong out – I do not know the challenger but he simply must get up. Twenty yards to go. Reality – it is not going to get up. Frankie's done it.

I stood on my stool, staring into the sky, not hearing a thing. It was like I was in a trance. It was probably about ten seconds, but time had stood still. I eventually turned back to look at the cheering crowds. Patrick and I stared at each other without speaking. I said, 'Patrick, can you handle the cash payout – I've got to go and sit in the car.' I later learned the final damage had been £23,000 on that race alone – £20,000 owed to the offices. Total loss on the day of £26,500. My previous biggest loss on any day during thirty years of on-course bookmaking had been £5,000.

Drove home with the staff in total silence. Everyone frightened to speak. Walked in the door, my wife greeted me in her normal cheery voice. 'Hello, darling – good day?'

'Dettori rode all seven winners,' I said.

'Fantastic,' she said, 'What a great achievement.'

I collapsed in my favourite chair, silently crying.

Many people have since said they think there was something strange about the race, and that 'they' let Frankie win. I do not believe this. It was his day, and on good days anybody can achieve anything. If it was to be his day he would have won the race whether it was the first or last race. It is the greatest achievement that ever will occur on such a competitive racecard.

During the next six months I was lucky enough to have a good run – mainly at Lingfield all-weather – which enabled me to pay off the offices, who were very patient with all on-course bookmakers, I believe. By February 1997 I had recovered. I was not in real danger of going under, as I had equities I could have cashed.

I often refer to that day with humour – but most of us on-course bookmakers pretended to put on a couldn't-care-less attitude when we had done our brains. It was to show everybody that we could easily cover the losses – whereas the truth was completely the opposite. With the passing years many stories about Frankie day get exaggerated, and jolly good stories they make. My own true story doesn't seem all that unusual now, but looking back at my financial records I now realize as he passed the post, I fleetingly thought, 'I've gone.'

Will Roseff is Managing Director of Wiltshire-based bookies Backhouse Racing, who offer hedging services to other bookmakers wanting to defray their potential losses or payouts. They also suffered:

We laid every bet we were asked for by our telephone clients, except those trade clients asking for prices in multiple bets, who were offered Starting Price instead. In doing so, we lost heaps – but most of the winners are still clients. Of course, all our cheques to the winners went out on Monday as usual. One of our phone clients was an ex-shop punter from Bristol, who had gradually gone blind. Deprived of the pleasure of studying the form, he had recently taken to backing jockeys' mounts. Luckily for him he chose Frankie that day. Luckily for us he didn't bother taking any prices. But he still copped over £10,000 for his 10p each-way Super Heinz. As he confided afterwards, all that form studying had never got him close to such a win. He is now in that great betting shop in the sky – but I doubt if he had many better days in this life than Dettori day.

A small, independent bookmaker with a couple of shops confessed to me, however, that his company had enjoyed a profitable day – by the simple expedient of laying off the biggest of their potential payouts, and receiving back from the bigger bookie a sum greater than that he had to hand over to his happy, if somewhat short-changed, punter.

Writing in the *Sporting Life* the day after the Magnificent Seven, under the headline 'Ascot Layers Blitzkrieged!', Doug Newton detailed the betting exchanges at the course on the day:

The ring has not seen anything like it for many a year. As Frankie Dettori swept through the card at Ascot yesterday he took the course bookies to the cleaners to the tune of around £1,400,000. As each race went to the Italian genius the layers losses kept mounting. The odds about each horse were slashed dramatically commensurate with their real formbook chances – but it was to no avail as the winners kept coming.

Things started off quietly. Wall Street's victory in the opener cost only around £30,000–£40,000, while Diffident attracted very little support before securing the Diadem Stakes at 12/1. Alarm bells started to ring in the trade offices before Mark of Esteem's Queen Elizabeth II victory. The Godolphin horse was the best backed, chiefly courtesy of office money, and landed bets worth over £100,000. After this, Decorated Hero was supported to 7/1 to take out £90,000. The offices decided enough was enough in the Rosemary Rated Stakes and plunged on Fatefully from 5/2 to 7/4 to the tune of well over £250,000 – while again in the following Blue Seal Stakes another £200,000 departed the satchels after Lochangel's win at 5/4.

It was the closing Gordon Carter Handicap which produced the craziest market moves, as layers gambled wildly against Dettori's mount, Fujiyama Crest – none more so than independent rails operator, Gary Wiltshire, who took on the ring. He said, 'You had to lay the horse at these prices – sadly it didn't come off.' Substantial bets for Fujiyama Crest produced nearly £600,000 liabilities and it was left to the gallant Wiltshire to sum up as he shouted: '9/4 Fujiyama – and 9/4 me for the Job Centre.'

Gary Wiltshire may have been speaking tongue in cheek but, as we have seen, both he and Barry Dennis had left themselves in highly vulnerable financial straits – a point picked up by off-course bookie and betting shop owner John Nelson, who had struggled to limit his potential losses by laying off as his usual sources proved reluctant to take his hedging bets. He had taken one 10p unit Lucky 63 bet which returned over £75,000, and faced a total loss of 'nearly £180,000' in accumulative bets alone – 'let alone the race-by race and across-the-card bets. I paid everybody,' he says, 'even though I had to get hold of money very quickly to do so.'

Several years later, Nelson – known as 'Sticks' in the trade – is still seething at some aspects of that afternoon, wondering how and why bookmakers on-course are able to accept potential liabilities which they may not be able to honour. When I spoke to him in March 2001 he'd just come back from Australia, 'where bookmakers on-course are tightly regulated,' he told me. 'They have to be prepared to accept bets of a certain size, but also prove they have the wherewithal to meet the payouts if necessary.'

So enraged was Nelson – once deputy chairman of the BBOA, and with over forty years' experience in bookmaking behind him – by the actions of the on-course bookies at Ascot on Dettori day that subsequently he went to Newmarket racecourse to confront them. 'I asked them what on earth they had been doing, and why the price of the last winner had not been shorter. I wanted to know how they could continue to take bets with no guarantee that they would be able to pay, and why the returned Starting Price did not reflect accurately the weight of money on the day – and I was almost beaten up for my pains. I wish some of those bookies had been wiped out financially,' he concludes, 'for the way in which they controlled and influenced the market that day. They had effectively turned from bookmakers into punters.'

Many would say that the line separating punter from bookie is as tenuous as that between love and hate. Nelson believes that on-course bookmakers should be obliged to operate under a system which ensures they are not tempted, or indeed permitted, to deliberately acquire liabilities which could sink them when they feel the odds are in their favour, and take bets without due regard to the possible consequences.

Gary Wiltshire would almost certainly take issue with John Nelson's analysis, although he did admit to me that he set off for Ascot that morning 'with £4,000'. He was, as we have seen, obliged to shell out rather more than that eventually, although he maintains 'we were winning up to the last two races'.

Wiltshire was financially ruined as a result. 'The house went, the cars, everything,' he told the *Evening Standard*'s Colin Fleetwood Jones in February 2001. 'I could have walked away without honouring my debts – betting debts are not recoverable by law – but that is not my way. If I'd done that I would have been warned off and never been able to go racing again – and I love the game.'

He refused to be bowed by his huge debts. 'I just got on with it. I sold Christmas paper in Oxford Street for a while, just to get a bit of money together. Then I stood at six horse race meetings and six greyhound fixtures every week, working every hour God made. I settled every bet. It added up to more than £800,000.' And he eventually fought his way back. 'I turned things around and moved out of the three-bedroomed property we'd taken in Birmingham to a bigger place near Stratford. I don't blame Frankie,' he told Ian Carnaby of *Sports Adviser*. 'I hope he rides a winner for me one day. The little devil owes me one.'

There is integrity in both Nelson's and Wiltshire's positions. On the one hand, Nelson's is a valid complaint – that to accept unlimited liabilities without the immediate means of settling them is unwise – and could feasibly have sparked nasty scenes that day had anyone who had been asked to wait for payment refused and demanded instant cash. Equally, it is true that there were no defaulters in the betting ring: they all paid, and a system developed over hundreds of years proved its worth under extreme pressure.

Wiltshire was on his way to Southwell races when we spoke about his often-reported comments that he would do the same thing again if a similar situation ever occurred. Was he serious? I received a less than convincing answer which suggested that, having had to work very hard to survive and return to the top, he would think very carefully before taking such a risk.

He said he had 'no hard feelings' about what happened that day. 'It did hurt me, but since that day people know me – it might be as the bookie who did his money, but the publicity has certainly helped to establish me.' He believes anyone suspicious about the running of the

Fujiyama Crest race is 'talking out of their pocket', an opinion he supports by hinting that, had the on-course bookies been at all concerned in advance about the conduct of the race, Frankie would definitely have gone off at long odds-on rather than 2/1. Wiltshire doubts whether we'll witness such a feat again.

IN 1996 SPREAD BETTING was still in its relative infancy. Five years on, and much more widely understood, it attracts a great deal more cash. But there was spread betting on Frankie's performances at Ascot that afternoon.

Wally Pyrah, traditional bookie turned spread convert, and the public voice of Sporting Index, told me about the performance index his company had run on Frankie, offering 25 points per winner, 10 points for a runner up, and 5 for a third. The company quoted a spread of 44–47 points. This represents their opinion of how well he might do, and means you can speculate on the total achieved being lower than 44, or higher than 47 – and, depending on which option you favour, you sell (lower) or buy (higher) for a unit stake of, perhaps, £1 a point.

Most punters who played chose to back Frankie to do well, one in particular buying at £50 per point. With a total of 175 points (25 points × seven races), the make-up, or final result, was 175 minus 47, or 128, which, at £50 per point, represented a return of £6,400. It is the nature of spread betting that it is possible to decide to close a bet as it progresses and the prevailing quote alters. So, although Sporting lost a reported £35,000, it would have faced far worse had half of their buyers not closed out with a 37 point profit as the line soared to 81–84 after the second race.

City Index, who had quoted Frankie's performance at 40–43, reported a £25,000 deficit.

But, compared with the fixed odds bookies, spread business was modest. William Hill Index's Mike Quigley was delighted to point out that, where Signor Dettori was concerned, his arm of the bookmaking empire had that afternoon, uniquely, traded at a profit: 'We took fifteen bets in total – nine of which were sellers, six buyers. Clients lost £7,307 and won £4,635, providing the company with a gross profit of £2,672 – to help counterbalance the millions lost in the rest of the organization!'

BOOKMAKERS STILL FEAR A repeat of the Magnificent Seven – it could happen again and, realistically, there is little that can be done to prevent another almighty hiding for the layers – after all, they cannot prevent punters from backing their favourite jockeys or trainers. Should similar mayhem occur in the near future, it is likely that the source will be Frankie again, or his National Hunt equivalent, Tony 'A.P.' McCoy and/or his employer, champion trainer Martin Pipe. The big bookies are, though, now far more aware of the possible danger. In *The Real McCoy*, his book about the leading jumps rider, Claude Duval quoted the response of Ladbrokes' Mike Dillon to Adrian Maguire's five winners at Kempton on 23 February 1997. 'Now Tony McCoy is the darling boy of the thousands of betting shop punters. He has reached the Lester Piggott status, in that gamblers will back his rides without even looking at the form, or the trainer, of his horses. They only have to see A.P. McCoy in the newspaper and they want to get on. The McCoy factor is now something we have become very much aware of daily.'

William Hill's David Hood was thinking along the same lines. A former jump jockey himself, who retired from the saddle in 1990, he admitted, 'Bookies now suffer from the Tony McCoy and Frankie Dettori factor. Punters look at their rides and back their horses no matter what the form or likely starting prices will be. If Tony McCoy ever went through the card at the Cheltenham Festival, it would cost the industry millions.' Shortly before Cheltenham's abandoned 2001 Festival meeting, McCoy landed the fourth five-timer (113/1) of his career, missing out just twice on a seven-race card at Warwick, on 17 February, with one of his losers, Rodock, a hot favourite.

The only real defence mechanisms for the industry are to be careful about the early price odds in the later races for a high-profile jockey with fancied runners earlier in the day, and to ensure that the appropriate hedging facilities and procedures are properly in place in the event of an alarm. Bookmakers know that a computerized system of calculating starting prices would offer them greater protection, but they are equally aware of the complete and implacable resistance even to the occasional floating of such an idea from punters and those who speak and write on their behalf. It is a long odds-against chance that a computerized starting price will be in place within the next few years.

DESPITE THE HUGE PAYOUTS earned by punters, there were nevertheless those who felt that the damage inflicted on the bookies could – and should – have been heavier. Writing in *Sports Adviser*, Dr Leighton Vaughan Williams, head of economic research at Nottingham Trent University, explained why:

> To a one pound stake, a seven horse Dettori accumulator yielded, at starting price, £25,000. At early prices, the same stake would have knocked back the bookmaker almost a quarter of a million.
>
> This tells a valuable tale. It is this. If you follow particular patterns or a particular system in placing multiple bets, beware if these patterns or your system is followed by others.
>
> For instance, you may back all the favourites at the televised meeting, or the leading trainer, or all the odds-on shots. Be wary of such an approach, however, because you can be sure that the bookmakers will be alert to it and will take defensive action.
>
> In the case of a series of horse races, the defence is to shorten up the starting prices of the tail end of potential winning multiples. If your accumulator bet is an obvious one, avoid it or at least be willing to accept miserly odds. At best, take the best prices, early on, before they become even more obvious than before. Because by the time the liabilities have mounted up, that quite healthy early price about the last leg of your Henry Cecil Newmarket accumulator may just have turned to 3/1 (if you're lucky). The result is that your potential winnings are halved, or worse. Of course, you might still be grateful for

the £25,000 to a pound, SP bettors won on Dettori day. Yet you could, by taking the early prices, have been earning that almost in annual interest!

Geoff Harvey, a betting writer and author of a book called *Successful Spread Betting*, also writes for *Sports Adviser* as 'our regular betting loophole spotter', and whereas Dr Williams warns against accumulative bets with obvious links, Harvey argues that this same factor can actually increase the value element of the wager:

The fundamental question on most punters' minds is *'How can I win a vast amount of money with minimum effort?'* Unfortunately, a definitive answer doesn't really exist yet, but there are a few types of accumulator bets that your bookie, if he realised the principle behind them, would probably prefer not to accept. They can be applied to a number of sports, but a good illustration cropped up during the most famous racing day in recent memory, when Frankie Dettori rode all seven winners at Ascot.

As each successive Dettori winner came in the big firms were desperately flinging money onto his mounts in an attempt to shorten up the SP. A lot of office money was running on Dettori horses in the form of multiple bets, hence the panic. Around £40 million was lost by the industry.

On the face of it a lot of small time punters, including one who made £550,000, simply had a fantastically lucky break. But dig into the mechanics of the betting that day and something very significant seems to emerge which just might help us emulate the feat of the few who suddenly became super rich.

Zero in on the events at Ascot around 5.20 on the glorious day. In ten minutes, Dettori was to ride Fujiyama Crest in the last race, looking to write himself into the history books. In the morning it had been available at 12/1, but in the betting ring 7/4 was the going price. At that point, which odds were the fairest reflection of the chances of Fujiyama Crest? Some might argue that 7/4 was ridiculously skinny – a false price influenced by the tidal wave of cash coming in on it. But should it have been as long as 12/1? It would be fair to say that Dettori's motivation was rather higher at that point than if it had just been the usual last race on the card. If we accept that the true odds were perhaps somewhere between the two, then there are interesting implications for some of those bets placed earlier in the day at the morning prices.

Turn the clock back to 11 a.m., and a semi-imaginary scene in a betting shop. A punter approaches the counter with a 50p accumulator on seven horses, with different jockeys at a mixture of meetings, i.e. the type of speculative bet that many indulge in. Should all seven succeed he will be paid at 200,000/1, though the true accumulative odds, if there was no bookies' margin, would be far in excess of this. For the bookies, it's money for old rope. Very infrequently such a bet will come off, but the bookie, sure that he has raked off a substantial margin, will be fine in the long run.

Behind him is our friend with 50p on all of Dettori's rides at Ascot. He takes as many early prices as possible, locking in the odds. This just seems like another mad speculative bet, but it is fundamentally different. In our look at Fujiyama Crest we have seen that the odds on at least one horse are affected by the performance of a previous one. As Dettori wins races the true chances of him following up seem to be increasing. The 50p accumulator is therefore, somewhat oddly, gaining in value as the afternoon wears on. From the bookies' point of view, this spells trouble.

On the day itself it was theoretically possible to take early prices to ensure accumulative odds in the region of 400,000/1 (an SP accumulator only returned 25,000/1). Though it is difficult to correctly assess the true chances of Dettori going through the card, it seems to me that the 50p accumulator (taking the early prices) was placed at abnormally advantageous odds. From our point of view the fact it won is actually rather academic – it is the possibility that the bet was good value to start with that is the important point.

In chasing the pot of gold I'm convinced that these types of 'hidden' related bets are worth pursuing. They are certainly much better than having some loose change on accumulators where there is no relationship at all between the legs of the bet.

These opposing views, from two undoubted experts in the field, highlight one of the enduringly fascinating questions about that last race: where was the value price in the betting? Was it – as hindsight suggests, because after all he went on to win the race – Fujiyama Crest, despite the predicted and readily available 12/1 odds having shrunk to 2/1? Would 12/1 have been value without the indirect influence on the race of the outcome of the previous six? Would 12/1 have been value if that race had been the first on the card? Was 2/1 any value at all when 12/1 had been available? Was the 2/1 excellent value when the weight of money suggested strongly that the true odds, in terms of the cash being thrown at the horse, would, in most circumstances, have resulted in odds of 1/4?

There is no conclusive answer to any of these thought-provoking conundrums, but it is worth perhaps considering some remarks by Irish professional bookmaker cum gambler, J.P. McManus, the owner of triple Champion Hurdler Istabraq, who figured briefly in our story as beaten favourite on the day Fujiyama Crest won the Gordon Carter in 1995. 'You should remember when you are winning,' says McManus, 'that there is another fellow losing, i.e. the bookmaker. He is just as affected by losing as is the punter. The bookmakers will start to chase their money, and that is when they offer better value as they are working to much tighter margins.'

Were the bookies chasing money in Fujiyama Crest's race and therefore forgetting the principles on which their art is based – make a book around the money you take, don't allow yourself to be overexposed to an unacceptable risk on just one runner?

McManus speaks of 'real professionals who always look for value, especially when the bookmakers are losing as they can possibly get a point or two over the odds. This doesn't often happen, but that is where the real professional, going with the streak, will hit the opposition when they are at their most vulnerable.' There was certainly a streak to go with that afternoon, but how many professionals were courageous enough to do just that? Some of them, from what I have been told, did the complete opposite and sided with the opposition in an effort to grab some of the action, misreading the signs, and misunderstanding just where the true value lay prior to the off of the 5.35 at Ascot.

The sole occasion on which I have rubbed shoulders with J.P. McManus could not have been a better demonstration of why he flourishes in a betting environment that ruthlessly destroys muddled and inflexible operators. It was at a London Racing Club evening when we were both at the bar to order drinks and McManus had asked the somewhat harassed barman for 'two mineral waters'. They had none, he was told. The great man did not miss a beat. 'Two large whiskies, then.'

I LEAVE THE LAST word, however, to Andrew Burke, a former betting-shop employee turned scourge of bookmakers, and the piece he wrote about that historic Ascot afternoon for specialist betting publication *Odds On*:

Permit me one belated observation on that wretched seven-timer: bugger. Months of my life, nay years, have been wasted hunched over form books. And I've paid the price. Straining to read the Gideon's Bible-sized print of *Timeform* has left me with premature myopia. And constantly leafing through the pages, from index to race, and race to index, has induced a swelling in my right arm diagnosed by a top Harley Street specialist as a form of RSI known as Punters' Wrist. Then there was all that time spent reading and re-reading Coton's books, and Mordin's books, and a dozen other instructional guides on how to make money from gambling. I even revisited an old school textbook on genetics, in the vain hope that it would help me better understand doseage and provide that missing vital edge. I'm still none the wiser. But if you have any questions on mutant DNA, give me a call. In fact, no matter what I do – apart from nicking the pens – I cannot inflict any damage whatsoever on anyone remotely associated with a bookmakers licence.

Meanwhile, somewhere in Britain, there is a middle-aged house-wife. A woman who, with several idle hours to fill between getting her hair done and the start of *Blind Date*, chose to back Frankie through the card because everyone knows the Spanish are good horsemen. Now she's about to add to the problems of over-crowding in Monaco.

Perhaps this is the secret. Burn those form books and forget the tipsters. Ignore the *Morning Line*. Watch the repeats of *Superman* instead. Empty your mind of all useless clutter, like knowledge, for instance. Have a stiff drink, stab the card with a sharp pin, and just wait for the cash to flood in.

CHAPTER THIRTEEN

'TAKEN IT FOR A RIDE'

ANAGRAM OF FRANKIE DETTORI

WHAT DO RACING FIGURES John McCririck and Lesley Graham (Channel 4's *Morning Line*), John Maxse (Jockey Club), Cornelius Lysaght (Radio 5 Live), Tom Clarke (*Sporting Life*), Tom Kelly (BOLA), Michael Caulfield (Jockeys Association) and myself have in common? Answer: we all, for one reason or another, missed most of Frankie's awesome afternoon. In John Maxse's case it was his father's birthday celebration. Tom Clarke was writing a speech. Lesley Graham can't remember what she *was* doing, but knows she wasn't following Frankie!

But a vast number of people certainly didn't miss the afternoon – and have remembered it very well ever since. So much so that when the *Observer*'s new Sport Monthly colour magazine polled readers in early 2001 to discover their '100 Most Memorable Sporting Moments', the Magnificent Seven soared into the top twenty, despite the fact that very few people actually witnessed the defining moment – the last race. Only those at the track – some 20,000 – or in betting shops, or with alternative access to the SIS TV coverage, were able to watch the action as it happened. Yet what they saw, and others heard or read about, made such a lasting impact that they placed it above such other iconic events as Gordon Banks' save against Pele (20th), Borg and McEnroe's 1981 Wimbledon tie-break (21st), Shane Warne's first Test ball to dismiss Mike Gatting (25th), Cantona's kung-fu kick (31st), Jonah Lomu's annihilation of England in 1995 (40th), Muhammad Ali lighting the Olympic flame (45th), Seb Coe's Moscow Olympic 1500m win (56th), the US team's Ryder Cup eighteenth-green invasion (82nd) and Eddie the Eagle in Olympic action (96th).

Among racing moments, only Red Rum's third Grand National victory in 1977 ranked higher, at 17th. Desert Orchid's Gold Cup was 30th, Devon Loch's Grand National fall 34th, Aldaniti's Grand National 67th, Foinavon's Grand National 77th and Shergar's Derby 85th. (In first place was Ian Botham's heroics in the 1981 Test against Australia, Manchester United's 1999 treble was second, and Gareth Edwards' 1973 try for the Barbarians against the All Blacks third.)

One can always find dissenting voices, even on the great occasion, and there are those prepared to stand against the overwhelming tide of praise, whether it be trainer David Elsworth, for whom 'Racing is not about turning jockeys into superstars – Frankie Dettori is a good jockey, but every time he farts he seems to make the front page', or Pete Nichols, author of BBC Radio 5 Live's *1997 Sports Yearbook*, for whom 'this wasn't quite the most astounding feat ever, because meetings used to be limited to six on a card, so most jockeys couldn't do it even if they wanted to.'

Frankie's afternoon's work earned him 'basic pay' of almost £16,000, according to the *Racing Post*. At that time, the paper explained, winning jockeys 'get about 4% of winnings. When broken down with the 4.02% for Pattern races and 4.34% for races with prize money down to 6th, Dettori is in line for £15,638 of the £384,992 accumulated by his seven successes.'

According to Ascot racecourse, however, his pay cheque amounted to £36,149.15 – over £2,500 per minute's competitive riding, as Frankie was actually 'working' for 13 minutes 25.25 seconds. No one knows which is correct, because top jocks like Frankie don't only get basic pay – but however much he pocketed, the sum took Dettori through the £2 million mark for his mount's earnings in Britain that year.

By an amazing coincidence, the total distance of the seven races he won was 7 miles, 7 furlongs.

Frankie's famous flying dismounts on the day caused the Jockey

Club to consider banning the practice, but they wisely thought better of it. 'We asked him not to jump off for safety reasons,' said Ascot's stewards' secretary, Patrick Hibbert-Foy. 'Some of us are of the opinion that it could be dangerous.' He had to admit, though, that there was nothing against it in the rules. 'I don't think we'll be introducing a new rule,' added David Pipe, the Jockey Club's Director of Public Affairs. 'There has been considerable concern from all sorts of people throughout racing, but Frankie has said that he will never do it if the horse he was riding had a suspect temperament, or was likely to have a problem with it.'

One consequence of his winning feat was that a seven-horse accumulator bet rapidly became known in the betting shops as a 'Dettori' – affording what a cross John McCririck dismisses as 'lazy hacks' the opportunity of coining a new cliché. 'They now start jumping up and down and shouting, "It's another Dettori!" when anyone even looks like riding a few winners on a card!'

In a letter to *The Times*, Terry Harper of Trowbridge in Wiltshire further suggested that 'as a bet on four selections in four races is known as a Yankee, perhaps a bet on seven selections in seven races should become a Frankie'. It didn't catch on.

In February 2001 Ascot racecourse was celebrating what it announced as 'Another Magnificent Seven'. *Sporting Life* reporter Gary Nutting was now supplying *Sportform*, an independent form guide, to the racecards of a number of major meetings. In his 'Top Tips' Gary gave seven selections for the races at Ascot's Mitsubishi Shogun Chase day. All seven won, at accumulative odds of over 20,000/1.

A website called Chance And Data in the News offered one of the more bizarre responses to the Magnificent Seven. 'Occasionally,' it observed, 'unusual sporting outcomes provide an opportunity to discuss some mathematics in an applied setting. Such is the case with the horse racing feat accomplished by Frankie Dettori.'

Depending on their out-of-school experiences, some students will easily understand the odds of 25,095/1 and the pay-out to the punter. Others will need some assistance. Unfortunately there is not enough information provided to work out the multiplicative effect of the seven races in determining the final odds.

Senior students who have considered the independence of events might like to consider whether they believe that the seven races constituted independent events. From the comment made by Dettori about the odds on his horse in the seventh race changing from 12/1 to 2/1, it would seem that the punters and bookmakers did not consider the races independent events. The formal relationship between odds and probability can be noted here.

The site then went on to set readers a series of questions arising out of the results, such as:

Do you think the seven races were 'independent' events?

If the odds on the last race changed from 12/1 to 2/1, what does this indicate about what the punters thought about the independence of the races?

In March 2001 the Labour Chancellor, Gordon Brown, announced that betting duty was to be abolished at the beginning of the following year. 'This has to rank alongside Red Rum's three Grand National wins and Frankie Dettori's Magnificent Seven as one of the best ever days for punters,' commented Ladbrokes' Chief Executive Chris Bell – confirmation that the phrase was now official shorthand for a gambler's bonanza of any kind.

IT WAS LITTLE WONDER that scores, if not hundreds, of racegoers at Ascot queued patiently that Saturday evening for Frankie to sign their racecards. Most would have wanted a personalized souvenir of the event, but sporting memorabilia is a booming market, and some racegoers – perhaps anticipating future riches by selling them on – even scoured rubbish bins for discarded cards. The jockey charged many of them a nominal £5 for the privilege, which then went to charity.

That day's Ascot racecard is indeed a piece of history in itself, if only because, for reasons not immediately evident, it had been generously sponsored by the Japan Association for International Horse Racing. As a result, racegoers were treated to a three-page spread on

'Pleasing the Fans in Japan', from which they learned that the Japanese are gaining 'greater free time to indulge pursuits such as camping and fishing', and especially enjoy betting on boat and bicycle racing, not to mention Japanese pinball. 'In recent years,' the good burghers of Berkshire were further informed, 'a special effort has been made to create interest in racing among young women' – the initiatives including 'cinema salons on horse racing, talk shows and tours of breeding farms'.

The cover features a photograph of Sheikh Mohammed's Blue Duster, ridden by Mick Kinane, winning the Group Three Queen Mary Stakes at Ascot in 1995 – and also a painting, whose identity proved more difficult to discover. Originally, Ascot told me that their maintenance team were 'looking for it in storage, as we have not found it on display', but eventually they came up trumps, having 'located the painting amongst our extensive archive!' It is a view of the Grandstand from 1840 by an artist who remains unknown – unless you know differently. Inside, this fascinating racecard also advises punters that 'the names of probable Riders, Weights, Pedigrees, Trainers' Names, Descriptions and Value of Races have been added for the convenience of the Public, but are not guaranteed as correct.' That's what I *call* a disclaimer!

One lucky fan grabbed a piece of racing history when Frankie Dettori threw his goggles into the crowd after his final winner. Others cherished the champagne stains on their clothes acquired during Frankie's bubbly-spraying celebrations.

No one can truly get under the skin of Frankie Dettori, but one racegoer managed the next best thing by snapping up the garment that allegedly had adorned his nether regions. Frankie's own turquoise underpants, as worn throughout his accomplishment of the Magnificent Seven, were later sold at auction to salesman Ken Knott for £2,500. Or were they? Mr Knott, a keen collector of sporting memorabilia, 'would not be amused,' my impeccable source informs me, 'to find out that he coughed up all this money for a pair of pants that weren't worn by Dettori on the day, but a pair fished out of a valet's bag.'

Whatever the truth of the matter, the beneficiaries of the sale were the Injured Jockeys' Fund, who organized the auction in memory of Richard Davis, the jump jockey who had died earlier that year. 'It's a real coup,' enthused Anna Baker-Creswell, one of the organizers, who could not disguise her delight at getting her hands inside Frankie's pants – 'How could you put a price on them?' Mr Knott outbid competitors including the *Daily Star* for the framed and autographed briefs, and pledged to hang them on the wall of his office. 'But,' queries my undercover, if not underwear, informant, 'could Dettori really have worn turquoise pants? What would his sponsor Yves St Laurent have to say about that?' I suspect this will remain a pants puzzle for the foreseeable future.

The Racing Museum at York boasts several Ascot artefacts from the day. There is a bookmaker's cheque from Coral for over £13,450.85 – cashed, one presumes – made out to fortunate Dettori punter A.J. Wilson from Doncaster, who staked just £2.13, together with a photocopy of his betting slip. Racing plates (the lightweight horseshoes worn during races) from six of the afternoon's winners are also on show, set on a velvet trimmed board – only Fujiyama Crest is missing. 'Unfortunately for you, David Nicholson rang on the morning after the race,' trainer Sir Michael Stoute's letter to the Museum explains, 'and I promised him one. The head lad and the lad that does the horse requested one each and I have kept one for myself.' Two 'flying dismount' photos of Frankie and a signed racecard complete the museum's display, which can be viewed at York racecourse on racedays or by special arrangement.

The saddlecloths carried by the seven winners – all signed by Frankie – turned up as Lot 38 at auction in a country pursuits sale at Sotheby's in London in March 2000, where they attracted a successful bid of £9,200 from Ascot racecourse. I'm not sure how they got to that sale, however, as Sotheby's were unable or unprepared to confirm who the vendor was.

But before you shell out a small fortune for something purporting to have a direct link with the historic occasion, listen to Brough Scott:

'I seem to have seen countless memorabilia from that day,' he ponders. 'If Frankie had used all the saddles that appear to have been auctioned, it should have been the Magnificent Seventy!'

David Osborne, from Enfield in North London, who was managing his betting shop in Cheshunt that Saturday and backed Ivor's Flutter to beat Fujiyama Crest, had a bright idea after the last race. 'The *Sporting Life* – God rest its soul – produced a laminated print of the following day's front page – pictures of Frankie, a big headline, Magnificent Seven. I thought, "Great, I'll get some framed, knock them out and earn a few quid." Well,' he told me in January 2001, 'I'm still looking at four of them. I managed to sell a couple. The best thing is, though, I took a couple to a boot sale and couldn't even get a fiver for them.'

Then, however, Osborne read that jump jockey Sharron Murgatroyd, paralysed in 1991 in a fall at Bangor, was holding an auction on behalf of the Midlands Centre for Spinal Injuries. He offered her one of his pictures, she got Frankie to sign it and auctioned it for £800. The winning bid came from Mair Stanyer, whose son Peter had been in the same ward of the Spinal Injuries Unit, following a car crash, as Sharron.

Michael J. Lester, from Ramsgate in Kent, told me about his own photographic souvenir of the day. Having won £100 on Mark of Esteem, he was in Ascot's paddock bar, where he met Godolphin Racing Manager Simon Crisford: 'I congratulated him, Godolphin and Frankie. Mr Crisford said, "It hasn't finished yet." "What, Fatefully in the next?" I asked, and he nodded. Our group then pooled our resources together and lumped the lot on. After watching in amazement as Frankie won the sixth and seventh, I bluffed my way into the jockeys' room and met the Great Man. Luckily, a professional racing photographer, David Hastings, was already there – and he took my photo with Frankie, his valet and a couple of other fellows who were working there. That photo now has pride of place amongst my collection of racing memorabilia.'

IN 1997 THE FINAL race on Ascot Festival Saturday was renamed The Magnificent Seven Gordon Carter Stakes, and Ascot's Douglas

Erskine-Crum revealed to me that to mark the fifth aniversary of the Magnificent Seven the course plans to unveil a life-sized sculpture of Frankie in flying dismount. A selection of memorabilia is scattered about the course, including the signed saddlecloths, displayed in its offices, and a framed portrait of Frankie with his winners, commissioned by Ascot and painted by Barry Linklater. The original painting for what became the first in a series of limited edition prints hangs in the Ascot Authority Luncheon Room, where VIP guests are entertained on racedays. Prints are on sale in the Ascot shop.

From early in 2002, the scene of Frankie's historic achievement will change forever when work begins on a major redevelopment of Ascot at a cost of £3.4 million. The straight mile course will be moved some 80 metres infield to slant across the jumps track, so that, following the Royal meeting in 2004, new grandstands can be built on its current site.

Ascot's Jason Brautigam found some more Magnificent memorabilia when in February 2001 he visited the Godolphin Gallery in Dubai – most notably, four horseshoes framed and displayed on the wall with photos of each of Godolphin's four winners that day. 'To be honest,' says Jason, 'I think they are a little peeved that Frankie's achievement has put Saeed bin Suroor's training feat in the shadows.'

Frankie lives in Stetchworth, not that far from Newmarket, home to the National Horse Racing Museum, which opened in 1983. It was perhaps that local connection which inspired Graham Snelling, the curator (even though he's a National Hunt fan himself!), to try and acquire the silks Dettori wore throughout that historic afternoon. Incredibly, by direct approaches to the relevant owners over several months, they were successful in doing so – and at no cost to the Museum. Graham says Fujiyama Crest's owner, Mr Hata, has already been to visit. The Museum's Frankie memorabilia, which also includes his riding boots from the day, is displayed in its Hall of Fame.

Frankie's whip, I was told, was auctioned for charity.

AT THE ASCOT MEETING that followed Frankie's Magnificent Seven, on 11 and 12 October 1996, its final flat fixture of the season,

Frankie arrived early in order to team up with Derek Thompson, who had wasted no time putting the wheels in motion to record a video tape reprising and analyzing the Magnificent Seven. 'That morning was incredible,' the ubiquitous, good-humoured Tommo told me. 'We walked up the track together, and he never stopped talking for about two and a half hours – we couldn't use all the material. He told me he wanted to get it all on tape, 'so I have something for my grandchildren'.

'He remembered everything [unlike Tommo himself, who, when I spoke to him, was initially under the impression that they'd recorded the video the day after the feat], all of it – exactly where he was during each race, and walking into the winner's enclosure with him was very, very special for me. It is one of my most cherished racing memories that Frankie agreed to record the video with me. I rank his achievement alongside Bob Champion and Aldaniti's Grand National.' That official video is on sale in the Ascot shop.

That same morning Frankie then went on to a special signing session to autograph copies of the Festival Saturday race programme, subsequently to be sold for £5 a time, with the entire proceeds donated to the Injured Jockeys' Fund. He was there for an hour – consequently arriving late in the weighing room for his first ride of the afternoon.

ONE YEAR AFTER THE great day, Frankie returned to Ascot on Festival Saturday 1997, again signing autographs, and also taking part in a photocall riding a donkey. 'This was seen as the only way,' explains Ascot's PR man Alistair Haggis, who organized it, 'the bookmakers could prevent him from doing the same again.'

After the fifth race, the saddle Dettori had used on the day, now mounted in a glass case, along with a Linklater print and a copy of *A Year In The Life of Frankie Dettori* was auctioned in the winner's enclosure by Barney Curley to raise money for his charity, Direct Aid for Africa, and did so the tune of £35,000 when Sheikh Mohammed outbid owner Michael Tabor.

Even five years down the track, mementoes are still available, though not quite in the financial league of Frankie's saddle. Available from British Sporting Heritage for 'today's extra special offer, just £49.95 including post and packaging', is a fine-art print in a limited edition of 950, showing a head and shoulders view of Frankie, right hand raised, surrounded by the seven heads of his winners. They've probably got one or two left in stock.

Even bookmakers William Hill, despite their seven-figure losses thanks to Frankie's seven winners, opted for commemoration rather than amnesia. The company had gritted its teeth and decided to acknowledge the significance of the event in its company Christmas card, which depicted six members of the board and senior management in various states of distress. MD John Brown was pouring himself a stiff drink. Financial controller Bob Lambert was scribbling out a pile of cheques. Shops supremo Liam McGuigan, a be-kilted Scot, was about to jump out of the window.

As a result, an Edinburgh punter who had scooped £57,000 from William Hill ended up with a unique piece of memorabilia. Liam McGuigan explains: 'I bumped into the big winner, an Italian called Toni, who had heard about the Christmas card, and asked whether I could get him one. I managed to persuade all six shown on the card to sign it for him – so he ended up with the only signed copy in existence.'

John Brown, meanwhile, bought himself a framed photo montage of Frankie's seven winners to be displayed in the company's box at Ascot – 'complete with a plaque saying "Limited Edition: £8 million."'

AND, FIVE YEARS ON, does the Magnificent Seven itself merit all this exhaustive commemoration? Just how great was Frankie's achievement? Let Brough Scott, himself formerly a quality jockey, go first:

> I rate it the greatest single riding achievement, the greatest single racing achievement – just about the greatest single sporting achievement that I have ever seen.

The force was with Frankie. Over the years I have been lucky enough to see a number of great jockeys in their pomp. At their best, whatever the difference in their style, they have shared one common characteristic – an almost tangible hunger for the post which brings an inevitability to the final outcome. Frankie had it that day for certain. To ride seven winners on that day, supposedly one of the most competitive cards in the calendar, and get everything right, is just impossible. I don't expect to see anything comparable again.

Simon Barnes is one of sport's great lateral thinkers. A man who knows sport inside out, but who reserves a special affection for sport involving horses – and someone who can be relied upon to approach an event from a different and invariably intriguing perspective. Simon began his analysis of the Frankie phenomenon for me with an emphatic observation I had heard several times before – that 'Frankie would never have won the seventh had it not been for the other six.' But he justified that conviction from an unexpected equine angle:

The interesting thing is why the other six made such a difference to the horse, who was presumably unaware of what had been going on – and it was the horse who ran faster than the others, not Frankie. It is a fascinating vignette of the communication between human and equine species. Frankie's surging confidence and desire inspired the horse to run the race of his life. It is the exact corollary to the truism that nervous riders make the horse nervous. The tensions of fear communicate in both directions; so do the tensions of confidence and desire. You can see it a million times on Newmarket Heath every morning: a calm lad on an oated-up skittering baby; and the lad wins because his calm overcomes the horse's fear. That race was a wonderful example of the jockey's confidence infecting the horse.

I think it was Fred Archer that said in defeat, 'I couldn't go without the horse, my Lord.' In this case, the horse couldn't have gone without the jockey. Horse-riding is not a question of where you put your arms and legs and body-weight. It is a communication of bodies, yes, but it is also a communication between minds. That last race was one of the more vivid examples of this savage communication.

There have been few better horsemen in racing history than John Francome, the former champion jump jockey called 'Greatest Jockey' only half in jest by John McCririck. Francome is suitably impressed with Frankie's feat:

If you're not riding with confidence after winning six, you never will be – it's like a striker who has already scored three goals winning a penalty – even if he never takes them he'll just demand the kick and stroke the ball in. He'd have won on a seaside donkey in the last. I don't think I ever had more than four winners in a day – but I would start sweating if I even had to ride that many on one day! When you stop to think about it as a jockey you say, what are the chances of getting seven rides to begin with? And then what are the chances of seven fancied rides on a card like that? It is almost unheard of.

But John felt that perhaps Frankie would have to share the historic honours with trainer Michael Dickinson, who sent out the first five in the Cheltenham Gold Cup in 1983: 'Somebody will ride seven on the card again before anyone trains the first five in the Gold Cup again.'

A champion jockey himself, Willie Carson watched Frankie in 'amazement' from the hospital bed where he was recovering from injury, and paid tribute to his 'great feat', but believes that 'all records are there to be broken. It's like lightning – it doesn't hit very often, but when it does it has a big impact.'

Trainer Mark Johnston was represented in that final race of the afternoon by Etterby Park. Five years on, though he has little recollection of his own horse, he can still remember the feeling that everyone was willing Frankie to win another: 'Of course, it could happen again,' he says, 'but it is very unlikely. I have no doubt that jockeys make a difference to horses, and one of the biggest factors is the confidence and will to win of the jockey. When jockeys get on a roll they win on horses that wouldn't otherwise do so, and that day Frankie was on the roll of all rolls.'

You or I might reasonably expect to remember with pride – or at least some kind of positive emotion – having had a horse running against Fujiyama Crest in that final race. So I was a little nonplussed when Juliana Abell wrote back that she and her husband David had not been represented. I checked my racecard again and there it said, quite clearly, that Sea Victor was owned by Mr J. David Abell and Mrs J. Abell. Assuming that the card was incorrect, I replied to Mrs Abell, telling her of the racecard error. 'You are right,' she wrote back, 'Sea Victor did run in Fujiyama Crest's race and I am mortified that I didn't remember this. Actually, he came last: there was something amiss. My memory gets a bit selective with disasters, because Sea Victor was by no means a useless horse and we never enter horses in races just because we want to see them run in a prestigious place.' It so happened, she added, that on 12 June of the same year Frankie had actually won on Sea Victor at Kempton for his sixth winner that day, which at that time was a record number of wins in one day for him – and a little dress rehearsal for 28 September.

Of course, the main reason why Mrs Abell had forgotten Sea Victor's sad performance was Frankie's achievement. 'The atmosphere that day was, of course, electric,' she recalled:

I particularly remember that Fujiyama Crest was an outsider who, under normal circumstances, could not have been expected to win the last race. Obviously neither of us have experienced a similar event in racing, since no one has ever matched Frankie's achievements. We were thrilled for him – we know him a little, and have never failed to find him delightful company, full of genuine charm. There are relatively few articulate professionals in racing, and Frankie is probably the best ambassador the sport has ever enjoyed in the whole of its history – quite apart from being one of its greatest jockeys.

'I have no doubt that it would not have been the same had it involved any other jockey,' says Geoff Lester of the *Sporting Life*. 'I am a great admirer of L. Piggott and P. Eddery, but neither has the charisma of Frankie – can you imagine them whipping up a storm and getting the crowd going after each winner? No way, Jose!' 'We've been waiting for a genuine, 24-carat hero for a while now,' commented Paul Haigh of the *Racing Post*, 'but it didn't occur to many of us that the hero might be one who could talk.' 'A sporting genius to compare with Pele, Ali and Lara', was the judgement of the *Guardian*'s Chris Hawkins. *Racehorses of 1996* devoted its cover to images of that afternoon. 'A magical man,' says Peter Bromley simply. 'One of the most remarkable landmarks in racing history,' is how Sir Peter O'Sullevan puts it.

Frankie himself seemed to have trouble getting the whole thing in perspective. 'I did not begin to understand what had happened. It was too much, too much,' he said afterwards. 'I wish I could go back and relive it again and milk it. I don't think anybody can explain what really happened,' he added, 'and neither can I.'

But perhaps he got nearer to the truth – and the magnitude of the achievement – when he reflected simply, 'God was on my side.'

CHAPTER FOURTEEN

'THE DAY DETTORI IS LOST FOR WORDS BOOKMAKERS WILL START
PAYING OUT ON LOSING HORSES'

JOHN KARTER

NEARLY FIVE YEARS AFTER his lifestyle-changing win,
Darren Yates, now thirty-four, was working in the business of
property renovation, both in the UK and in Spain, where he
had bought himself a villa. The Dettori money certainly altered
the direction of his life significantly.

First, he handed out a six-figure sum from his winnings to
others. He also upped his betting stakes sharply, and initially made it
pay – landing £68,000 with a Trixie bet. But then, in a single afternoon, he gambled away £42,000.

That brought him back down to earth with a start. 'I had a few big
bets after The Win,' he told me, 'and within six weeks I was over
£40,000 up – but I blew it all in one day at York when, although I'd
always made it a rule never to back odds-on shots, I backed two of
them, and they both lost.' I had heard on the racing rumour-rounds
that Darren's betting patterns had begun to cause some concern –
after all, it would have been poor PR for the industry if the biggest
single winner on Dettori day had within a few weeks given it all back
to the bookies. A few words from the right people, and his own real-
ization that he risked squandering the enviable future handed to him
literally on a racing plate, had the desired effect. Darren reconsidered
his approach to betting and reverted to more modest outlays.

He dabbled in racehorse ownership – but his first two investments,
the 10,000-guinea yearling appropriately named Seventh Heaven and
Torianna, both trained by Jack Berry, proved singularly unsuccessful. But
finally, on 26 August 1998, Royal Dome won a modest sixteen-runner

race at Carlisle at rewarding odds of 25/1 to give Darren his first winner as an owner. Royal Dome was successful again, on 30 September at Newcastle, at 14/1, again beating fifteen rivals. Then Natsmagirl, named in honour of daughter Natalie, won for him at Thirsk at 4/1 on 15 June 1999, but in many attempts never managed to repeat the feat.

When I spoke to Darren, though, he was without a horse to his name – for reasons that would have endeared him to sheikhs and wealthy owners throughout the land. 'The prize money is a joke,' he sniffed. 'There's no point being in it.' Since when, I have to ask – well, I would, wouldn't I – have people been able to expect a profit from their own private hobbies?

He and Annaley – 'her objections to my betting were played up by the media for the sake of their stories' – have since doubled the size of their family, with the addition of Bradley, now three. The football playing has now been dropped in favour of squash and scuba-diving, and Darren is adamant that early retirement beckons – vowing to work flat out for the next few years before calling it a day at forty-five.

And what is his opinion of that fateful last race which made his fortune? 'At the time I was caught up in the excitement,' he muses. 'I have since watched it a few times – I've got the video – and although many people have said to me, "Pat Eddery let him win!" there's no way – he leathered his horse to try to beat Frankie!' It's OK, Darren – we won't be asking for the money back!

MARY BOLTON DID TELL me that they had invested their money wisely and resisted the temptation to indulge John's ambition to have a horse in training with Henry Cecil – 'He's always been John's hero, but he's way out of our price league.' She and John have attended every Ascot Festival meeting since, and although she still has the occasional flutter, she is realistic enough not to back only Frankie's mounts. 'When we go racing, Frankie still remembers and gives us a wave.'

THE SEVEN HORSES ON which Frankie rode to his Magnificent achievement subsequently went on to mixed fortunes. Wall Street did not race again in the UK, turning out next at Woodbine in Canada in October 1996 and finishing eighth of fifteen.

Diffident's next outing, over 7 furlongs at Doncaster, was to be his last win in this country, though the *Racing Post* reported that he won the National Day Cup at Abu Dhabi in 1997, before going to stud in India.

Mark of Esteem was subsequently sent off to America to run in the Breeders' Cup Mile at Woodbine in October, but disappointed there and was returned to the Dalham Hall Stud to stand at a fee of £20,000.

Decorated Hero was retired as a seven-year-old in July 1999 owing to injury. By then he had won fourteen races and over £300,000 in winner's prize money, with victories in Britain, France, California and Hong Kong. Frankie won eight times on him and nicknamed him 'Square Wheels': 'He was a really great character and was always a very kind and gentle horse.' On Ascot Festival Saturday in 2000, horse and jockey were reunited in the winner's enclosure and then, before the race they'd won together, the Tote Festival Handicap, paraded in front of the stands. At the time of writing, Decorated Hero was residing at the British Racing School in Newmarket where Ascot Racecourse was sponsoring his stable.

Frankie teamed up with Fatefully again next time out at Ascot in October and they were 8/11 winners. Fatefully raced on until October 1997, failing to win again in six additional attempts.

Lochangel was retired in September 1999, having only won twice more in eighteen attempts, albeit usually competing in decent company. Frankie paid tribute: 'Lochangel was one of the last of my Magnificent Seven still to be racing, so it's very sad she's been retired. I'll never forget her – that's for certain.' She won £180,000 in prize money.

Although Julian Wilson's earlier overture to Martin Pipe had come to naught, Fujiyama Crest did eventually switch codes and go jumping – though stable lad Derek Heeney continued to keep tabs on his equine pal. Sold for 69,000 guineas to go hurdling with trainer

Nicky Henderson, the horse was badly injured, however, when slipping off the ramp of his horsebox. He recovered to win at Stratford under Richard Dunwoody in May 1998, then went point-to-pointing with little success, and finally reverted to the flat. But he never threatened to hit the heights again, despite landing a 12/1 win partnered by John Lowe in June 2000 in a modest claiming race at Nottingham. That was his penultimate race; the last of thirty-six outings under Rules (eight wins in all) was also at Nottingham the following month, when Lowe again rode him, this time into fifth place of nine runners.

One evening at Sandown later in the year Derek Heeney saw Frankie. 'How's the old horse?' the jockey called out, and indicated that he might be interested in buying him. Derek passed on to Frankie's then-agent, Peter Burrell, the information from the horse's trainer, Roger Curtis, that Fujiyama was available for £2,000, and on Halloween night eight-year-old Fujiyama Crest arrived with the Dettoris to begin a new life as a hack for Frankie's wife, Catherine.

'This horse made me famous, so giving him a home for the rest of his life is the least I can do.' Frankie plans to leave Fujiyama to enjoy himself until the fifth anniversary of his great day – 'Then we'll see about getting him back in shape to be ridden.'

WHEN FRANKIE DETTORI ARRIVED at Ascot racecourse on Saturday 28 September 1996, he was the current champion jockey – albeit unlikely to retain his title after an injury-hit season. He was extremely well known, liked and respected within the racing fraternity, but a peripheral figure on the wider domestic sporting scene and a mere bit part player on the worldwide stage. A few hours later he departed from Ascot as the newest UK sporting superstar – more, indeed, than that, according to *The Times*, which, in terms designed to turn the head of even the most well-adjusted individual, would declare in a leader column just two days on, 'To win seven races in an afternoon turns men into gods'.

Divine or otherwise, Dettori's life could never be the same again. 'This achievement catapulted him into the mainstream media,'

Barney Curley remarked to me, 'which has traditionally proved very hard for racing figures to achieve.' The Jockeysroom.com website declared Frankie to be 'probably the most recognised man on a horse anywhere in the world since Clint Eastwood and John Wayne'. For *Total Sport* magazine he was 'the first rock 'n' roll jockey.' Even the then Prime Minister, John Major, probably mindful that his constituency of Huntingdon included a racecourse, wanted to bask in some reflected glory. Just five days after the event, Frankie was invited to a Downing Street reception for sporting achievers. All of a sudden, everyone, everywhere, knew about him – and what's more they liked him, even though he was only an honorary Brit!

But, of course, Frankie had come to us. He'd wanted to be one of us. Unlike, perhaps, many high profile footballers, tennis players, boxers and athletes, he hadn't come here chasing the cash. He'd worked his way painstakingly and uncomplainingly up the hard way, and for that we took to him. Indeed, that day at Ascot we probably began to love him – and, leaving aside the odd curmudgeonly critic, we still do.

There lies the difference between Dettori and the greatest jockey to precede him. Everyone recognized and respected Lester Piggott, but almost no one – outside his immediate family – could claim with a straight face to love him. An unapproachable, single-minded, stand-offish figure with a minor speech impediment, you could never envisage him as a media friendly character. Frankie, by contrast, was young, funny, attractive to women, non-threatening, and cool with other men. Paul Haigh of the *Racing Post* described him as 'a man who embraces success like an old chum and controls any tendency to self-adoration with frequent references to what he has plenty of reason to regard as a benevolent deity'. He adds that 'he isn't in the slightest bit self-conscious about the joy that victory brings him and isn't in the slightest bit grudging about sharing that joy'. And he had single-handedly inflicted more misery on Public Enemy Number One – the bookmaking business – in a single afternoon than any other individual throughout history.

FRANKIE BECAME UBIQUITOUS – AND was so clearly having a great time that no one could resent it. Whether he could ever have achieved such status had he stayed in Italy is doubtful. Giancarlo Galavotti, a writer for *La Gazzetta dello Sport*, told me, 'Frankie's popularity in England is a million times wider. Flat racing in Italy is very limited – I can't say the impact there of the Magnificent Seven was beyond newspaper reports on the day and mentions on the news bulletins.' Elsewhere, though, the impact was significant. Roger Wright, formerly Racing Editor of the Press Association news and sports agency, told me what big news the Magnificent Seven had been out in Singapore, where he'd been working for the *Straits Times*. 'They were particularly impressed,' he added, 'by the quality of the races involved.'

Dettori's rapport with the younger generation – many of them too young legally to have placed so much as the smallest flutter on one of his mounts – was evident when he presented *Top of the Pops* a few weeks later. The only surprise is that he didn't have a single of his own to promote. Subsequently he appeared on Clive Anderson's show, and on *TFI Friday* with Chris Evans, where he caused quite a sensation by performing a party-trick levitation stunt which ended with him leaping out of a box, having appeared to hover in mid-air.

The extent of his popularity was demonstrated at the end of the year when he was voted into third place in the BBC TV Sports Personality of the Year Award, beaten only by the winner, Damon Hill and runner-up, Steve Redgrave (how unjustified that order seems now). It was the best performance by a jockey in the forty-two-year history of the prestigious event. He also landed his third consecutive Lord Derby Award as Jockey of the Year, presented annually at the Horse Race Writers Awards luncheon.

On 20 March 1997, according to Woodrow Wyatt's *Journal*, 'it was the opening of the flat season. We were making an announcement that the charming little Frankie Dettori (jockey) will promote the Tote.' Note how he appears to be one of the few people in the entire universe who believes that readers will need to be told who Dettori is:

'We have to pay him £50,000,' Wyatt went on, 'with an option to take him on for another two years. But he is well worth it.'

In *The Racing Tribe*, her insightful book about the various factions that patronise racecourses, anthropologist Kate Fox muses wryly on the essence of Dettori's reputation:

> Many of the more frosty old-school-tie tribal elders, who initially frowned on Frankie's flying dismounts and other uninhibited antics, have gradually succumbed and now look on with indulgent, avuncular smiles. Frankie has been officially declared Good For Racing, and has accordingly been granted a sort of diplomatic immunity from traditionalist censure. In the superstitious minds of the Racing Tribe, he is more than just an effective ambassador; he represents racing not just as a spokesman, but as a tribal icon. To express disapproval of racing's lucky charm would be to invite divine retribution.

On 20 July 1997 Frankie married Catherine – the pair had met when she was leading up a filly for him at Haydock.

As the 1997 Ascot Festival drew near, the media began to crank up stories about whether Frankie could possibly repeat the Magnificent Seven – but it seemed more than a little doubtful since he only had six mounts booked for the first day. Enter Claude Duval, our friend, the 'Punters' Pal' of the *Sun*, who takes up the story:

> A year after Frankie Dettori's Magnificent Seven he had six booked rides at the same meeting but a blank in the Tote Festival Handicap. Enjoying a glass – or two – of claret with Peter 'The Voice' O'Sullevan after a Carbine Club racing lunch in London, the great man suggested, 'I'm sure that the *Sun* can put that right.' Peter's idea clicked and within minutes I had contacted trainer Brian Meehan and leased Tumbleweed Ridge for the day. All other daily papers and the *Racing Post* had lead stories that Dettori could not repeat his seven as he did not have a ride in the big handicap. We kept back the story for our early editions and then splashed the back page with the Dettori news.
>
> Sadly, Tumbleweed Ridge did not trouble the judge but he made the 'Italian Stallion' as I call him, and a group of *Sun* readers, very

happy. I will not forget the wisecracks Dettori had with the *Sun* readers before the race and his engaging personality. Racing is lucky to have such an ambassador.

Claude is right – Tumbleweed Ridge, a 12/1 chance, didn't justify the faith shown in him – trailing home, tailed off, last of the twenty-five runners in the Tote Festival Handicap, the fourth race on the card at Ascot on Saturday 27 September 1997.

But it had taken no longer than the very first race for history not to repeat itself. Frankie was on the unfancied King Sound, trained by John Gosden; it drifted from 7/1 to 10/1 in the Cumberland Lodge Stakes, but ran on well to finish third. At this point the nation's news hacks immediately lost interest. Russian Revival (John Gosden) then started as 3/1 favourite for the Racal Diadem Stakes, but could manage only fourth place. Allied Forces (Saeed bin Suroor), 9/2, never looked likely to win the Queen Elizabeth II Stake and beat only three other runners home. After Tumbleweed Ridge disappointed, Frankie fared a little better on John Gosden's Noisette, the 9/2 second favourite in the Rosemary Rated Stakes Handicap, which plugged on to take third of eleven. Then Atuf (Saeed bin Suroor) nearly broke Frankie's duck in the Blue Seal Conditions Stakes, but after drifting from 9/4 to 4/1 had to settle for second behind 14/1 shot Wenda.

Like all good showmen, though, Frankie was determined to send 'em home happy. In 'his' race, the now re-named 'Magnificent Seven' Gordon Carter Stakes (Handicap), he duly rewarded the faithful as 9/2 chance Jaseur, owned by Sheikh Mohammed, ran on well to win by three and a half lengths. This time Frankie didn't win from the front but came through with just over 2 furlongs to go. It was his third consecutive win in the race, and Ascot's Douglas Erskine-Crum later told me that Frankie was using a special gold-coloured saddle given to him by a fan, which, I understand, was subsequently auctioned.

That win sharpened Frankie's appetite for winners and he opened the Sunday of the Festival with an 8/13 victory on Mudeer, scored at 10/1 in the fourth on Glorosia and closed out in the last by completing his treble on 11/8 favourite Puce – the shade the bookies were once more beginning to turn.

IN 1998 THE 150TH edition of the 'top people's' index, *Who's Who*, was published – and Frankie was in it – squeezed between Sir Dermot Humphrey de Trafford and the Reverend Canon Andrew Gilchrist Deuchar. The entry divulged the little known fact that Frankie's mother's maiden name was Nieman. Also in there was Frankie's father-in-law, Professor William Richard (Twink) Allen, PhD, ScD, since 1995 Professor of Equine Reproduction at the University of Cambridge.

In 1997 Frankie rode 176 winners, to finish runner-up in the title race, and in 1998 he rode 132 to occupy the same position. But no one can enjoy permanent upward momentum, and in the 1998 Breeders Cup meeting on 7 November, one of the most valuable day's racing anywhere in the world, Frankie's first setback since Ascot occurred. The Classic was the world's richest-ever single race, with a $5.12 million purse, and Frankie was riding the Godolphin horse Swain. There with every chance and just a couple of furlongs to go, Dettori seemed to lose control and uncharacteristically gave Swain a very hard ride, allowing Pat Day on Awesome Again to win. In the official *Breeders Cup Statistics* publication, the incident is neatly encapsulated: 'In deep stretch, Swain bore out badly under Dettori's whip. Silver Charm also drifted out creating a hole for Awesome Again to come charging through.' Second was Kentucky Derby winner Silver Charm, and the Godolphin runner came in third. 'An absolute stinker', was the BBC website's verdict on Frankie's performance. 'Dettori beat Swain across the track in the Classic with a whipping frenzy which almost certainly denied the partnership success in the most prestigious race on the card,' declared Richard Edmondson in the *Independent*. 'His reputation was subsequently lynched in the American media,' added the journalist, 'and it took some while for Frankie to distance the whole memory.' One American racing fan, Dan Stoicheff, dubbed Dettori and other European riders as 'jerkeys'. In fact, for some while Frankie seemed to be in a state of self-denial, refusing grimly – against all the television evidence – to accept he had done anything wrong, and seeking stubbornly to justify his performance. 'In racing,' Dettori himself is once reputed to have remarked, 'it helps to be a good bullshitter – you must have the ability to make excuses' – which perhaps gives an insight into his reaction. I remember watching that race live with my best friend Graham Brown, a man who loves and knows his racing, and at the end of it looking at each other and agreeing that this was not Frankie's finest hour.

Tony Stafford, the perceptive racing correspondent of the *Daily Telegraph*, went straight to the probable source of Frankie's setback. 'The sudden success of two championships, and then the Ascot seven-timer, seemed to reduce Dettori's hunger for racing, and he tended to be blasé about some of the lesser days.' But the Swain incident, Stafford believed, lanced this developing boil: 'a period of contrition followed'.

In the autumn Frankie courted controversy when he admitted to having taken diuretic drugs in the past to keep his weight down. There was only one day's racing at the Ascot Festival – Saturday had to be abandoned because the course was waterlogged – and of the nine races run on the Sunday, Frankie won three.

Before the year was out, Frankie redeemed his previous Breeders Cup debacle by winning the identical race on Daylami. He yelled at the crowd in triumph, pumping his arms and leaping off the horse – looking 'like a prisoner suddenly set free', observed *Sports Illustrated*'s William Nack. On the way to weigh in he stopped to drink a beer handed to him by a fan. Afterwards, he was a man unburdened. 'Revenge is a plate you eat cold,' he reflected enigmatically, 'and mine was freezing. Everybody tried to kill me last year. OK, I made a mistake, but don't judge me on one ride.' He again rode 132 domestic winners, but finished only third in the title race. He rounded the year off by becoming the proud father of a son, Leo, born on 4 October.

THEN CAME THE TRAUMATIC incident that cemented his place in the affections of the entire nation, and tinged his reputation with an almost mystical sense of indestructibility.

On 1 June 2000 Frankie and fellow jockey Ray Cochrane set off to fly from Newmarket to Goodwood racecourse in a Piper Seneca light aircraft. Just after take-off the plane nose-dived, crashed and caught fire. 'Before the impact I didn't scream,' Dettori was to recall, 'because I didn't think there was any point. I knew that I was going to die.'

Cochrane rescued Frankie from the burning wreck, but was unable to free the pilot, Patrick Mackey, who perished. Subsequently Cochrane would be awarded a Silver Medal by the Royal Humane Society for his actions following the crash. Both jockeys were treated in Addenbrookes Hospital in Cambridge, Frankie for a broken ankle, damaged ribs and facial injuries, Cochrane for injuries to his back, arms and face.

Incredibly, Cochrane was back in the saddle only seven weeks later, riding the well backed 7/4 favourite Glowing to victory in the Fund for Addenbrookes Fillies Handicap at Newmarket. Shortly after, though, he announced his retirement from the saddle, and for the 2001 season Frankie appointed him as his riding agent. 'He took me under his wing when I was a youngster at Luca Cumani's and we went through hell and back together with the plane crash,' Dettori explained. 'It is the least I can do for him after everything he has done for me.'

Frankie himself returned to the track on 5 August 2000 – also, ironically, at Newmarket. 'I got to the start in the first race and tried to collect my thoughts,' he said afterwards, 'and I just glanced towards the two wooden huts by the ditch. I said, "Hello, ditch," and I froze for a few seconds and my thoughts went to the accident and to poor Patrick.' To no one's great surprise – except, again, the on-course bookies – he completed a 10/1 double on his two comeback rides, on 11/4 joint favourite Atlantis Prince in the Tote Exacta Conditions Stakes, and on Dim Sums in the Tote Scoop 6 Nursery. He'd 'done' the layers again, and in the process won the bonus fund of the Scoop 6 for a syndicate, landing them about £1.4 million.

The crash, he admitted, changed his perspective on life. He was no longer prepared to neglect his home and family life in favour of rushing around to regain the jockey's championship. With a healthy income from sponsorship deals – a six-figure deal with Yves Saint Laurent and a range of oven-ready, healthy-eating food for the supermarkets – he is hardly on the breadline. But in a major interview with Brough Scott in the *Sunday Telegraph* that September, he rounded on the criticism his realignment of priorities had attracted. 'I hear it all the time,' he exploded, 'all this "part-time jockey" and "not hungry" bollocks. What do they expect me to do today? Drive all the way to Beverley, six hours in the car, to ride perhaps one winner and just about lose money on the day?'

In August 2000 plans were announced for a feature film of Frankie's life. The movie, to be co-produced by *Birds of a Feather* star Pauline Quirke's production company, Quirky Film and Television, would 'focus on the day when Frankie rode seven winners at Ascot and how that affected those who betted, as well as him'. The plane crash would also feature prominently. Frankie, who was not expected to play himself, would act as 'a technical and racing consultant'. It is hard, it must be said, to think of a good film about the world of horse racing – but I suppose there is always a first time!

Also in August, Frankie and the whole Godolphin team were devastated by the career ending injury suffered by Dubai Millennium, regarded by them as the best horse they – and, indeed, anyone else – had ever been privileged to be associated with.

In October Frankie again broke new ground for a jockey when he addressed the Oxford Union, giving a ten-minute talk on his career before inviting questions. The illustrious line of former speakers in whose footsteps he was following includes Nelson Mandela and Ronald Reagan – though neither, it is believed, performed a flying dismount from a table in the library! Meanwhile, Sheikh Mohammed used his delivery of the important Gimcrack Speech to racing folk to address the Frankie factor. 'We in Dubai are not a betting people,' he said, 'but I understand well how vital, and indeed central, betting is to the racing public. I understand that when they cheer Frankie Dettori into the winner's enclosure it is not just because he is a popular and refreshing figure, but because they have had a bet on him as well.'

In the New Year's Honours List at the end of 2000 Frankie was awarded an honorary MBE, a tribute reserved for those from overseas who have excelled within their fields in Britain. It was presented to him at Sandown in April 2001 by the Foreign Secretary, Robin Cook. 'This is just a congratulation for what I did for my sport,' he told Radio 5 Live's Robin Bailey. 'The seven winners that day – we've had racing for 280 years and it's never been done before. It's something I'm very proud of, and that's a special day I'll never forget.' By now Frankie had ridden a total of 1,649 winners in Britain.

The year 2001 brought Dettori a varied record of 'firsts'. Frankie and Catherine celebrated the arrival of their second child, a daughter named Ella. He appeared in a TV advertisement for Lloyds TSB in which he was asked what he would bank given the chance. 'All the things I'm not allowed to eat,' replies Dettori, whom camera trickery then reveals to be about thirty stone in weight. In Dubai he was pictured with Tiger Woods at the Emirates Golf Club, where the world number one was contesting the Dubai Open.

But in Dubai he also came an unexpected cropper – twice. Victorious in the Maktoum Challenge at Nad El Sheba in February – his first racecourse appearance of the year, having recently had the surgical screws removed from the ankle injured in the plane crash – he treated the crowd to a traditional flying dismount – only, for the first time in public, to fall over on landing. And in March he had another rare taste of critical displeasure when he failed to ride a winner during the Dubai World Cup evening – the meeting he himself had dubbed 'the equine Olympics'. After returning a well beaten eighth on Best of the Bests, Godolphin's chief World Cup hope, Dettori was booed by some sections of the crowd. 'I was disappointed,' reflected a philosophical Frankie, 'but I guess they all had him as a banker in the Pick Seven, which is the only bet you can have in Dubai, and Best of the Bests was the last leg! You can't please everyone.' No, but it is significant that again he should deflect any suggestion of his riding performance being at fault. Even the greats cannot enjoy permanent praise, and are sure to be mightily disappointed sooner rather than later if they choose to overlook this harsh fact of life.

FRANKIE HAS PLENTY OF years in hand – although he did tell Brough Scott recently that he envisaged retirement in 2010. He doesn't fancy becoming a trainer: 'There's no point swapping one twenty-four hours a day, seven days a week job for another.' TV and media work appeals much more. But while he has opted no longer to chase the jockey championship, he thinks nothing of a schedule which, in just a few days in April 2001, saw him race in Hong Kong, Italy, Germany and the UK.

What motivates him to continue racing? I suspect that, like that great record breaker and undisputed best-of-his-generation Sir Gordon Richards, he is desperate to consolidate his place in racing history by winning the most prestigious horse race of all: the Derby. It is the only English Classic to have eluded him. 'Every year I get a little more pressure,' he has said. 'I would like to get my name on that list.' Sir Gordon, who first became champion jockey in 1925, did not win the Derby until 1953, with his twenty-eighth and final mount in the race, Pinza. 'Pete Sampras has said that if he wins Wimbledon again, he might well retire on court – could you do that if you do finally win the Derby?' I asked Frankie. 'I could see myself announcing my retirement there and then,' he replied, before qualifying his answer. 'Although then I'd definitely want to ride the horse in the rest of his races.' Eventually Frankie Dettori will close that one remaining gap in his already outrageously impressive record, and when he does, quit or not, it will be yet another Magnificent achievement.

BIBLIOGRAPHY

Bradley, Graham, *The Wayward Lad*, Green Water, 2000

Cope's Racegoers Encyclopaedia 1958, Copes Publications, 1958

Costello, John & Finnegan, Pat, *Tapestry of Turf*, Moa, 1988

Curley, Barney & Townsend, Nick, *Giving A Little Back*, Collins Willow, 1998

Dettori, Frankie, *A Year In The Life of Frankie Dettori*, Heinemann, 1996

Directory of the Turf 1996, Kilijaro, 1996

English, Alan (ed.), *Sunday Times Sporting Century*, Collins Willow, 1999

50 Years of Sports Report, Collins Willow, 1997

Fox, Kate, *The Racing Tribe*, Metro, 1999

Hammond, Gerald, *Horse Racing: A Book of Words*, Carcanet, 1992

Karter, John, *Frankie Dettori: The Illustrated Biography*, Headline, 1995

Krone, Julie, *Riding For My Life*, Little, Brown & Co., 1995

Lucas, Pat, *Fifty Years of Racing At Chepstow*, H.G. Walters, 1976

McCoy, Tony with Duval, Claude, *The Real McCoy: My Life So Far*, Hodder & Stoughton, 1998

McCririck, John, *John McCririck's World of Betting*, Stanley Paul, 1991

Morris, Tony & Randall, John, *Horse Racing: Records, Facts and Champions*, Guinness, 1990

Mortimer, Roger, Onslow, Richard, & Willett, Peter, *Biographical Encyclopaedia of British Flat Racing*, Macdonald & Jane's, 1978

Nichols, Pete, *BBC Radio 5 Live Sports Yearbook 1997*, Oddball, 1996

Pitt, Chris, *A Long Time Gone*, Portway Press, 1996

Randall, John & Morris, Tony, *Century of Champions*, Portway Press, 1999

Richards, Gordon, *My Story*, Hodder & Stoughton, 1955

Sharpe, Graham, *William Hill's Racing Dates*, Virgin, 1993

————————, *Coups and Cons*, Rowton Press, 1991

Smith, Doug & Willett, Peter, *Five Times Champion*, Pelham, 1968

Smith, Raymond, *The High Rollers of the Turf*, Sporting Book Publishers, 1992

Stafford, Tony, *Racehorses of 1996* (Timeform) Pocket Racing Guide, Collins Willow, 2000

Tanner, Michael, *Great Jockeys Of The Flat*, Guinness, 1992

Thompson, Derek & Cameron, C., *Tommo's Year*, Boxtree, 1997

Walwyn, Peter, *Handy All the Way*,
Metro Books, 2000

Ward, Andrew, *Horse Racing's Strangest
Races*, Robson, 2000

Welch, David (ed.), *Daily Telegraph
Century of Sport*, Macmillan, 1999

Wilson, Julian, *Some You Win*, Collins
Willow, 1998

Wyatt, Woodrow, *The Journals of
Woodrow Wyatt, Volume 3*,
Macmillan, 2000

VIDEO

Frankie Dettori's Magnificent Seven,
Race Vision, 1996

Frankie Dettori Horsing Around, VCI,
1998

MISCELLANY

FRANKIE FILE

Born 15 December 1970, Milan

Height 5ft 4in

Wife Catherine (daughter of
Cambridge University Professor
Twink Allen), wed 20 July 1997.

Children Leo, Ella

Supports Arsenal, Juventus

Likes Cooking, good wine, golf

Dislikes Cold weather, travelling,
being late, fatty foods, 'living 14lbs
below natural body weight'

Heroes Angel Cordero, Steve Cauthen,
Ayrton Senna

Food Pasta

Drink Champagne, Bordeaux

Clothes Smart suits, tracksuits

Car Audi S8, Ferrari

Champion Jockey 1994 (233 winners),
1995 (216 winners)

Hosted *Top of the Pops* after his
Magnificent Seven; BBC TV Sports
Personality of the Year Award, 3rd,
1996; Derby Awards (Media
decided Jockey of Year 1994, 1995,
1996)

First winner Rif (Turin, 16 Nov 1986)

First British winner Lizzy Hare
(Goodwood, 9 June 1987)

First Royal Ascot winner Mark of
Distinction (Queen Anne Stakes,
1990)

UK winners (except where noted) 1986 –
16 (all in Italy); 1987 – 8;
1988 – 22; 1989 – 75; 1990 – 141;
1991 – 94; 1992 – 101; 1993 – 149
(runner-up); 1994 – 233
(Champion); 1995 – 216
(Champion); 1996 – 123 (5th);
1997 – 176 (runner-up); 1998 – 132
(runner-up); 1999 – 132 (3rd);
2000 – 47 (from 247 rides, prize
money £1,324,141.68)

ACKNOWLEDGEMENTS

BEFORE THE PROJECT EVENTUALLY came to fruition, a couple of people over the last couple of years suggested to me that I write a book about Frankie Dettori's Magnificent Seven. Derek McGovern, formerly Sports Editor of the *Racing Post*, raised the idea of our collaborating on one, and Paul Ridley, then Sports Editor of the *Sun*, for which Frankie Dettori was a columnist, suggested such a project would be worthwhile, as we watched England play Brazil at Wembley Stadium.

But, though I have had some twenty books published before, and despite my being the sponsor and organizer of the William Hill Sports Book of the Year award, it took Bill McCreadie of Aurum Press to decide to give it a go – probably out of sheer boredom during a lunch I spent trying to get him to publish a book I wanted to write about the history of betting shops.

In researching the book I endeavoured to speak to people across the whole spectrum of the racing and betting industries. The majority were instantly forthcoming and helpful with their memories, thoughts and opinions. Some wanted nothing to do with me – well, Luca Cumani never did have much time for bookies, or 'leeches' as he likes to call us, and J.A. McGrath obviously had much better things to do. I had to resort to bribery to get a few words out of Pat Eddery.

But the likes of Ray Cochrane, Willie Carson, Kevin Darley, John Francome, John McCririck, Jim McGrath, Barry Dennis, Barney Curley, Claude Duval (the 'Punter's Pal' at the *Sun*), Derek Thompson, Lesley Graham, Clare Balding, Mark Johnston, Sir Peter O'Sullevan, Sir Michael Stoute, Julian Wilson, Gary Wiltshire and Neal Wilkins were all of inestimable assistance. Ed Chamberlain at Sports Advisor, Kate Fox, and Tim Exell of Green Umbrella permitted the use of information vital to the overview of the day. Claude Duval and Brough Scott could not have been more helpful had they been writing books of their own.

I spoke to or corresponded with many journalists, owners,

punters, racegoers, bookmakers and betting-shop staff, who responded with invaluable personal memories of the day that added great colour to the bare facts, and I'm very grateful to every one of them.

Jon Lees, formerly of the Press Association and currently with the *Racing Post*, and a long-standing and much-valued friend, came up trumps by readily agreeing to check through and proofread the pages for me and thus helped eliminate glaring errors. Jason Brautigam at Ascot chased down a whole lot of irritating yet vital racecourse facts for me. My friends Neil Crespin, Gary Nutting and fellow Wealdstone FC supporter Howard Krais – who loaned me his treasured Magnificent Seven-day racecard – all helped sustain the months of graft and grind which went into building up a balanced picture of how a remarkable day unfolded, and how it affected so many people in so many ways.

And, after a false start which resulted in my chatting to his spoof answerphone message, Frankie himself was generous enough to confront a couple of provocative questions.

One or two sources requested, and have been granted, anonymity – of course that can diminish the authority of their contributions, but if it is the only way of addressing a point or incident, then so be it. Finally, I have no doubt that the achievement described in this book is one of the most astounding, outrageously unlikely, yet wholly deserved individual feats of sporting genius to occur in my lifetime.

Graham Sharpe, March 2001
(on board the Orient Express)

GLOSSARY

Accumulator	bet involving more than one selection in which all selections must win to give a pay-out
Across-the-card	selections running at different meetings in races timed within fifteen minutes of each other
Bins	slang for binoculars
Canadian	also known as a Super Yankee – bet consisting of five selections in twenty-six different combinations of doubles, trebles and accumulators
Each-Way	bet in which half of the total stake is invested on a selection to win, with the remaining half on a selection to finish placed – usually 1st, 2nd or 3rd
Early Bird prices	those offered on selected races in advance of race-course betting getting underway
Even-money	odds where winnings are equal to the original stake
Field-book	bookies' record of bets struck on an event or race.
Form book	a record of the horses' performance in previous races
Hedging	bookie's way of reducing potential liability by placing a bet on the same outcome for themselves
Heinz	Bet incorporating 57 bets, involving 6 selections in different races – 15 doubles, 20 trebles, 15 four-folds, 6 fivefolds, 1 sixfold
Layer	bookmaker
Laying off	bookmaker passing on all or part of a bet to another bookie
Odds against	odds greater than even money
Odds on	odds shorter than even money
Over-broke	betting without a profit margin
Over-round	betting with a built-in profit margin
Penalty	additional weight allotted in a future race to a horse that has won last time out.

Pitch	position from which a racecourse bookie conducts business
Price	odds offered by a bookmaker
Punter	gambler
Rails	bookmakers' pitches on the rail separating different racecourse enclosures
Readies	cash
Return	amount – winnings plus stake – paid out to winning punters.
Ring	bookies with pitches in the main betting enclosure of a racecourse
Running-on money	accumulating potential pay-out from a bet with more than one selection
Show	list of odds for a particular race
Starting Price	odds arrived at by taking average prices available in the racecourse betting ring
Super Heinz	bet consisting of seven selections in total of 120 doubles, trebles and different accumulators
Tissue	advance betting forecast prepared for racecourse bookies
Tote	government controlled racecourse pool betting system
Trade clients	bookmaker clients of other bookmakers
Weighed in	after race check to ensure a jockey has carried the correct weight during a race
Yankee	accumulative wager involving four selections